stickyfaith
Teen Curriculum

stickyfaith
Teen Curriculum

10 lessons to
nurture faith beyond
high school

Dr. Kara E. Powell
Brad M. Griffin

ZONDERVAN®

ZONDERVAN.com/
AUTHORTRACKER
follow your favorite authors

ZONDERVAN

Sticky Faith Teen Curriculum

Copyright © 2011 by Kara E. Powell and Brad M. Griffin

YS Youth Specialties is a trademark of YOUTHWORKS!, INCORPORATED
and is registered with the United States Patent and Trademark Office.

This title is also available as a Zondervan ebook.
Visit www.zondervan.com/ebooks.

Requests for information should be addressed to:

Zondervan, *Grand Rapids, Michigan 49530*

ISBN 978-0-310-88926-7

Cover direction: Tammy Johnson
Cover photography: Reflex Stock
Interior design: Ben Fetterley and Matt Van Zomeren

Printed in the United States of America

14 15 16 17 18 /DCI/ 22 21 20 19 18 17 16 15 14 13 12 11 10 9 8 7 6 5

contents

introduction

When it comes to preparing seniors for life after youth group, these are probably the two most important statistics you need to know:

45 percent and 16 percent.

Approximately 40 to 50 percent of youth group seniors significantly struggle with their faith and with finding a church after graduation.[1]

Only about 16 percent of college freshmen felt well prepared by their youth ministries for what they encountered after graduation.[2]

For us though, this curriculum is about more than numbers. It's about real students—students just like the ones in your ministry right now.

This curriculum is about students like this one who described the overall challenge of transitioning from high school to college:

> [It's] like you're leaving on a giant cruise ship. You're heading out of this harbor, and everyone's waving you off. Let's say this ship is your faith. As soon as you start sailing out to this new port called *college*, you realize you're in a dingy. You don't have this huge ship, and you're completely not prepared, and your boat is sinking! Unless there's someone with a life raft who's ready to say, "We got you. Come right here. This is where you can be, and this is where you can grow," you're done.

The Sticky Faith Movement

Through our mission of leveraging research into resources that elevate leaders, kids, and families, we at the

Real Reflections from Real Students

Graduation is exciting, but also it's really scary—and it's okay to be scared, it's okay to be nervous . . . but jump in with both feet!

Fuller Youth Institute (FYI) want to partner with you to offer kids a stronger "ship" of faith and extend a life raft to those who feel like they're drowning.

In 2004 FYI launched the College Transition Project, a study of nearly 500 American youth group graduates during their transition to college. The goals of this project were to better understand the dynamics of life after youth group and to pinpoint steps that parents, youth leaders, churches, and students themselves could take to help launch students on trajectories of lifelong faith and service.

What started as a handful of research initiatives has become a movement—a movement of churches, parents, grandparents, youth leaders, children's leaders, and senior pastors who want to help students' faith not merely survive, but thrive, after high school.

Defining Sticky Faith

The goal of this curriculum is—quite simply—to help teenagers develop Sticky Faith. By "Sticky Faith" we mean a combination of characteristics, all of which exist in a dynamic tension . . .

> *Faith that's internalized and externalized:* a faith that's part of a student's thoughts and emotions, and is externalized through choices and actions that reflect that faith commitment. These behaviors include regular attendance in a church/campus group, prayer and Bible reading, service to others, and lower participation in risky behaviors, in particular sex and alcohol consumption. In other words, Sticky Faith involves whole-person life integration, at least to some degree.
>
> *Faith that's personal[3] and communal*: a faith that celebrates God's specific care for each person while always locating faith in the global and local church community.
>
> *Faith that's mature and maturing*: a faith that shows marks of spiritual maturity but is also in the growth process. We don't assume a high school senior or college freshman (or a youth worker for that matter) will have a completely "mature" faith. We're all in process.

Putting it in even simpler terms, the vast majority of students we interviewed—even those who had thrived in college—reported that college had been both a growing and a challenging experience. Much of that growth and challenge came from the new experiences and perspectives students encountered after graduation. Reading through the transcripts, it seems that the typical college student sits down at a table full of new and interesting worldviews and people; and instead of faith being merely one of many voices clamoring for attention around the table, those with Sticky Faith had determined that their faith would sit at the head of the table.

> For more on the questions we asked, please visit www.stickyfaith.org.

The Two-Word Glue of Sticky Faith

Based on our research and our ongoing theological reflection, if we were asked to summarize the glue that creates Sticky Faith in two words, it would be *gospel* and *identity*.

Gospel, of course, is literally the "good news" of God's Kingdom plan of saving us and transforming us into Kingdom people through the death and resurrection of Jesus Christ.

Identity is a bit harder to nail down. Quite simply, it's a mix of what we think about ourselves and what others think and portray *to us* about ourselves, which inevitably influences—if not determines—the choices we make and the way we relate to God and to others. Our identity development is a process; one that started when we took our first breaths and will end when we take our last ones.

We cover the gospel and identity extensively in sessions one and two. But we also encourage you to strengthen the gospel and identity threads that weave their way through this entire curriculum. To help you do that, we have strategically sprinkled "gospel" and "identity" discussion questions and learning activities throughout the other eight sessions.

In particular, session two ("How Do I See Myself after Graduation?"), invites students to complete a handout titled **Identity That Sticks** that helps them dream about who they want to be—or their identities—a year from now. Since identity formation is a process, we have tied that particular activity into later sessions so students can continue to edit and expand their views of who God wants them to be after graduation. Therefore we encourage you to collect the **Identity That Sticks** handouts from your students after they've filled them out; then, every time you reintroduce the concept of identity during subsequent discussions, give back the **Identity That Sticks** handouts to your students so they can add to them. We'll make all of this clear in the pages that follow, but we wanted to give you a heads-up now.

Why This Curriculum Is Important

One of the questions we most regularly asked youth group graduates was, "What advice would you give youth leaders when it comes to their graduating seniors?" Their top piece of advice by far was to spend time better preparing seniors for all they would face after graduation. Nothing else came close.

Hence this curriculum.

Six Ways to Get the Most Out of This Sticky Faith Resource . . .

1. Realize (and celebrate) that this curriculum is a mix of Scripture and social science data, a combination of theology and research. Bible-based theology is the heartbeat of this curriculum, but good research conducted by the Fuller Youth Institute and other research centers also pulses throughout. Throughout the sessions we've sprinkled quotes from youth group graduates we've surveyed that you can read yourself or share with your group if you'd like.

2. As much as you can, don't force your students to make the Sticky Faith commitments you want them to make. These are seniors, and you've trained them well to think and come to their own conclusions. The students in our study with the most mature faith had wrestled with important faith questions until they came up with their own answers.

3. Relax. Know that this curriculum doesn't require a lot of preparation or props. You're dealing with seniors, not seventh-graders. The goal is to have deep, provocative, authentic, practical discussions that are also fun

and lively. But you won't need marshmallows or inner tubes to make them happen.

4. Understand the **Now, New, How** format of each session. Following the pattern of some of our previous books . . .[4]

   Now helps you and your students discuss what is, and isn't, happening now.

   New brings fresh insights from Scripture, research, and experience (yours and your students').

   How prompts your seniors to translate their new insights into new patterns in their own lives.

5. Customize these sessions to fit your seniors. We know students, but we don't know *your* students. We've offered a suggested order, but feel free to cut, add, and reshuffle the deck of sessions to develop a Sticky Faith game plan that best fits your ministry.

   On that note, we've geared each session to last approximately 60 to 90 minutes, but we've also sprinkled **Have More Time?** and **More Worship and Prayer** activities throughout this curriculum that you can add or use instead of what we've suggested.

6. Be creative with how you use this curriculum. Some groups do one session per month for the school year; others have waited until January and launched a more intensive series in the winter and spring of the senior year. Still others choose to dive deep into this curriculum during weekend retreats or overnighters.

Above the Research

As much as we wish there were a foolproof curriculum to build Sticky Faith, we will be the first to admit that there isn't. There is no Sticky Faith silver bullet, and there is no

Real Reflections from Real Students

Don't be afraid to challenge teens in ways that may seem beyond realistic at first. Too often we expect so little from junior highers and high schoolers. We think that they're at a low level and just won't comprehend, so we don't ask very difficult questions and dumb down things or make smaller challenges that seem easier and more realistic. But that leaves them either bored or unprepared for the real questions they're going to face when they get to college.

simple list of steps you can take to give students a faith that lasts. Part of what makes youth ministry so demanding is that there are rarely easy answers.

While that may sound discouraging, let us make a few additional admissions that will hopefully encourage you.

As much as we love research, we will also be the first to admit that we love God more.

As much as we believe in research, we will also quickly admit that we believe in God more.

As a result of our research, our nationwide conversations with kids and leaders, and even our ministry experience, we have learned much about Sticky Faith. This curriculum is full of suggestions. But our top suggestion is this: Trust God with your kids and continue to ask—maybe at times beg—God to build Sticky Faith in them.

Here's to Sticky Faith!

Along with this senior curriculum, we (and a few others) have written two additional books out of our Sticky Faith research. One is for youth workers, titled *Sticky Faith: Youth Worker Edition*; the other is for parents of teenagers, titled *Sticky Faith* (yes, we were super creative with the titles). If you like this curriculum and want more ideas for how to equip kids and their parents for nurturing long-term faith, please check out these other books.

1

what's the real gospel?

The Big Idea:

The real gospel is centered on grace, not works.

You'll Need:

Copies of the **10 Things I Do to Live Like a Christian** handout on page 20

Poster paper

Tape

Pens or pencils

Markers

A Red Bull drink (or another similarly highly caffeinated beverage)

Copies of the **Ephesians 2:1-10** handout on page 21. Ahead of time, follow the guidelines on this handout so you can display your own version of the passage, complete with colorful markings and notes.

Colored pencils and/or highlighters

Copies of the **When I Blow It** handout on page 22

Bibles

More Worship and Prayer: Copies of the **God's Face** handout on page 23

Optional: If you decide to watch the video "What You Need to Know about Grace" on the DVD, be sure to figure out ahead of time how you'll show the video (laptop, projector, etc.) and set up accordingly. Alternatively you could send students a link to the video later to watch as a follow-up to the session.

NOW

Start by saying: **Recent research indicates that up to half of youth group seniors will drift from their faith in the first year after graduation. Does this surprise you?**

Explain as you distribute pencils and copies of the **10 Things I Do to Live Like a Christian** handout: **Today we're going to look at how your faith impacts your life currently. On this handout I want you to make a list of up to 10 things that you do to live like a Christian.**

As students are making their lists, tape a sheet of poster paper and write at the top: "Things I Do to Live Like a Christian."

After students have finished, ask each to share two or three items from their lists. Write down what they share on the sheet of poster paper.

Ask: **What stands out to you about what we've listed?**

NOTE: In a few minutes, you'll help students understand that making a list like this misses the heart of Christianity, which isn't about us "being good" but much more about God's goodness to us. A few of your more theologically astute seniors might point this out now, before you're ready to share that principle with the whole group. If they do, try to redirect them toward writing down or discussing what we're supposed to "do to live like a Christian" by saying something like, **You're right that grace is important, but right now we're focusing on what we each do to live like a Christian.**

Ask: **Is a list like this helpful to your faith or not?**

Continue: **According to one study of 500 high school graduates, students who said "no" to alcohol and sex before high school graduation ended up saying "yes" after getting to college.**

Raise a can of Red Bull (or another favorite energy drink, in which case you can shift the metaphor in the next paragraph) and ask: **What are the highs and lows of energy drinks like this?** Students will likely share that Red Bull makes them feel great at first but soon the caffeine and sugar wear off and they crash. Hard.

Continue: **Too many of us have bought into a Red Bull Gospel. It might help us make good decisions at first, but the Red Bull Gospel doesn't lead to Sticky Faith. It's not deep enough to help us say "no" and "yes" to the right things after we graduate.**

NEW

Explain: **While Red Bull wasn't invented until recently, from Paul's letter to the Ephesians we see he was dealing with his own version of the Red Bull Gospel in the first century.**

We'll read 10 verses of this letter together in a format that might be new to you.

Distribute copies of the **Ephesians 2:1-10** handout to your students, making sure you read aloud the guidelines at the top of the handout. If you've worked through the passage ahead of time, show students your colorful version of Ephesians 2 as a model of what they might do themselves.

Give your students plenty of time to read, and reread, the passage, noting themes, opposing phrases, or questions the passage

Scripture Sidebar

The city of Ephesus was at an intersection of major trade routes and was thus an important commercial center in western Asia Minor (now Turkey). For three years, Paul made Ephesus a center for evangelism, and the church thrived.

What makes the letter to the Ephesians different from many of Paul's other epistles is that it doesn't address any particular theological error or heresy. Instead Paul seems concerned with helping the believers in Ephesus understand some basic Christian beliefs.

raises for them. After students are finished, lead them through the manuscript study with questions like:

What words or phrases does Paul repeat?
What words or phrases are opposites?
What are Paul's most important ideas?
What questions does this passage raise for you?

Feel free to interject the following into your discussion:

The "death" that Paul describes in Ephesians 2:1 doesn't refer only to physical death—the "death" that folks (apart from Jesus) experience after their lives end. It refers to a real death right now since the most vital part of a person—the spirit—is dead apart from Jesus.

Interestingly, Paul includes himself in the "all of us" who are disobedient and dead apart from Christ in Ephesians 2:3. Paul teaches in Romans 3:23 that "all have sinned and fall short of the glory of God," and he backs that up in this Ephesians passage by including himself in the category of people who need Jesus to rescue them from sin.

The "grace" that Paul describes in the passage is God's free gift to us—and applies both to our earthly and eternal lives—which God offers us through Christ.

The "works" in verse 9 refer to deeds or activities we do in a futile attempt to save ourselves (apart from God's grace); the "works" in verse 10 refer to the ways we obey God in our daily actions, as a sign of our gratitude for salvation.

The root word for *created* in verse 10 is "ktizo" (pronounced kuh-TIDZ-oh) and is only used in the Greek language when referring to God. What's special about the way God creates?

The word for *handiwork* in verse 10 is "poiema" (pronounced poe-AY-ma), which means "work of art" in Greek. What do you think it means to be God's work of art?

Sometimes it may seem as though Paul's writings are all about grace and the book of James is all about works. As we see from Ephesians 2:1-10, Paul's theology is grounded in grace, but then he encourages believers to serve out of gratitude for their salvation. If we assume Paul and James are teaching different messages, then we probably aren't reading them carefully enough.

One of the main points, if not *the* main point, that you want students to get from this passage is the relationship between works and salvation. We don't do good works in order to experience salvation; it's because of our salvation that we do good works. And by doing those good works, we become human pieces of art—living masterpieces—of God.

Ask: **What does it mean to live as God's handiwork, and how is that different than simply "being a good person"?**

At this point remove the poster paper list of **Things I Do to Live Like a Christian** from the wall and rip it up. Ask your students to do the same with the lists they've made.

Ask: **How do you feel now that you've torn up the list?**

Continue: The reality is that there *are* things we *do* as people who follow Jesus, but none of them are at the heart of the gospel that leads to Sticky Faith.

HOW

Research found that Christian kids who fail to do the items on our "10 Things" lists feel guilty and hypocritical. For instance, if they decide to party, they don't feel like they can show up at church or on-campus Christian groups because folks there know they've been partying. As a result, they end up turning away from God and Christian community.

Ask: How should the Ephesians passage make a difference to the Christian student who wakes up after a night of making some mistakes?

Have More Time?

At this point, you might want to show the "What You Need to Know about Grace" video found on the resource DVD. You might set it up by saying something like, **Here's what a few other youth leaders have to say about God's grace.** Afterward, invite students to share their responses to the video by asking a question such as, **What emotions or thoughts did that stir in you? What resonates with our discussion about grace so far? How is this different from how you might have understood grace in the past?**

Distribute copies of **When I Blow It** to your students as you explain: **Odds**

Real Reflections from Real Students

You've got to find a campus ministry or a church that's going to be real about stuff. You don't want to walk into a church or college ministry where everyone is fake. You want to be able to walk in and say, "Yeah, I was at a party this weekend, and I drank too much . . ." You gotta find people you can be real with. Because if you walk into a college ministry, and it's just full of fake people you can't be honest with, then you're sunk.

are good that you'll blow it in some way after you graduate. So I want us to think now about what we'll do when we mess up. Give students a few minutes to complete their handouts.

If you have time, close by singing a familiar song or two about grace. If you're short on time, simply close in prayer, thanking God for freedom and a gospel based not in what we do for God, but in what God has done for us through Jesus.

More Worship and Prayer

The Face of God

The final discussion paragraphs on "blowing it" might stir a lot of feelings in students who already feel like they've completely blown it with God. Similarly, some students may be feeling like they "get it" for the first time as you talk about the gospel of grace. The following idea for a closing prayer may be something you want to plan time for, particularly if you're anticipating that your students may need more space for reflection. If it's natural for your setting, you may want to include musical worship in this reflection time. You also may want to allow students to simply spend time in silence.

Explain: **The good news is that God's grace knows no bounds. While grace is more fully explained in the New Testament, it also threads its way through the Old Testament. One of those powerful Old Testament threads is the idea of *blessing*. In the Old Testament, God's unfailing love and care is closely connected with God's blessing.**

In Numbers 6:24-26, the Lord gives Moses specific instructions for how the priests of Israel were to bless—in New Testament terms, *show God's grace*—to God's people. This blessing is still widely used in churches today:

The Lord bless you
and keep you;
the Lord make his face shine on you
and be gracious to you;
the Lord turn his face toward you
and give you peace.

It's interesting that God's face is mentioned *twice* in this blessing—that the Lord would "make his face shine on" and "turn his face toward" the people. These expressions imply God showering grace on his creation.

Distribute the **God's Face** handout and invite students to read the Numbers 6 passage a few times and reflect silently on the handout questions. When they're finished, close by reading aloud Numbers 6:24-26 as a benediction—a sending prayer—that you say on behalf of your students.

10 THINGS I DO TO LIVE LIKE A CHRISTIAN

In the space below, write down up to 10 things you do to live like a Christian. Try to be as specific as possible. For example, instead of writing down "pray," write down "I try to remember to pray as I'm driving to school in the morning."

1.

2.

3.

4.

5.

6.

7.

8.

9.

10.

EPHESIANS 2:1-10

Read the Scripture text once. Then read it again, this time circling, underlining, or drawing arrows with different colored pencils toward the following:

Themes you notice, either because the same words are used or the same concepts are used

Opposite phrases or concepts

Ideas that seem important to the author

Ideas that are important to you

Questions this passage raises for you

Then try reading the passage a third, and even a fourth, time. New insights might stand out to you each time you read it.

[1]As for you, you were dead in your transgressions and sins, [2]in which you used to live when you followed the ways of this world and of the ruler of the kingdom of the air, the spirit who is now at work in those who are disobedient. [3]All of us also lived among them at one time, gratifying the cravings of our flesh and following its desires and thoughts. Like the rest, we were by nature deserving of wrath. [4]But because of his great love for us, God, who is rich in mercy, [5]made us alive with Christ even when we were dead in transgressions—it is by grace you have been saved. [6]And God raised us up with Christ and seated us with him in the heavenly realms in Christ Jesus, [7]in order that in the coming ages he might show the incomparable riches of his grace, expressed in his kindness to us in Christ Jesus. [8]For it is by grace you have been saved, through faith—and this is not from your-selves, it is the gift of God—[9]not by works, so that no one can boast. [10]For we are God's handiwork, created in Christ Jesus to do good works, which God prepared in advance for us to do.

WHEN I BLOW IT

When I blow it, either before or after I graduate, I want to remember the gospel that Paul describes in Ephesians 2:1-10.

How do my sins and mistakes resemble death? (Ephesians 2:1)

How can I experience the grace that saves me from my sin? (Ephesians 2:5)

How can I now help my life reflect "God's handiwork" and the "good works, which God prepared in advance for us to do"? (Ephesians 2:10)

Who can I talk to about the mistakes that I make?

If I could have a conversation with God, what do I think God would say to me about my mistakes—ones I've already made, and ones I'm going to make?

GOD'S FACE

The Lord bless you
   and keep you;
the Lord make his face shine on you
   and be gracious to you;
the Lord turn his face toward you
   and give you peace.

> Numbers 6:24-26

Questions for Individual Prayer and Reflection

When you consider God's face turned toward you, what expression do you see? What expression do you imagine might be on God's face right now? If it's hard to imagine God's face shining on you, what do you suppose could be the reason?

Think for a moment about God's face turned toward—not away from—each of us. Whether we do all the stuff on our "Live Like a Christian" list or blow it all, God sees and loves us. How does that make you feel? What questions does it raise?

2

how do i see myself
after graduation?

The Big Idea:

*Having a scripturally informed view of
our identities will help us keep our faith at
the center of who we are and what we do.*

You'll Need:

To wear two layers of shirts (i.e., a T-shirt plus an outer shirt or
    sweatshirt)
Pens or pencils
Have More Time? Items: Crayons, markers, or other art supplies
Index cards
Copies of the **God's Vision for My Identity** handout on page 31
Copies of the **Identity That Sticks** handout on pages 32–33
A small safe or lockbox, or if that's not possible, a suitcase
    or briefcase you can seal with a buckle, zipper, or button snap
A mailing envelope for each student
Bibles

More Worship and Prayer: Copies of the **Naming** handout on page 34
Optional: If you decide to watch parts 1 and 2 of the video "Karis'
Story" found on the resource DVD, be sure to figure out ahead of
time how you'll show the video (laptop, projector, etc.) and set up
accordingly.

NOW

Start by having students pick two words that help describe who they've been in high school, and briefly share why they picked them. For example, "*baseball* and *friends*, because I played baseball a lot and my friends mean the most to me."

Transition to a deeper level of conversation: **I'm glad we've gotten to know each other a bit more. Now I want to take us to a deeper level. I want you to think about how you view yourself—beyond just what you do and what you like.**

Distribute an index card and pencil/pen to each student so that students can write their own thoughts on their index cards. Explain: **I'd like you to write "I am" at the top of the index card, and then I want you to make a list of the words that come to your mind that help you complete that thought as quickly as you can.** As students are writing, you should also write your own list of "I am" words.

After students have finished their lists, continue by asking rhetorically: **I'm curious where your faith fell on your lists. Was it toward the top? Somewhere in the middle? Toward the end? Or maybe even left off your list?**

   As we learn together about Sticky Faith, today we're going to spend some time thinking about our identities—meaning a mix of what we think about ourselves and what others think and portray *to us* about ourselves.

Ask: **How do you think we who follow Jesus view our identities differently than folks who don't?**

Research shows that right after seniors graduate high school, they often encounter new situations that seem to clash with who they were in high school.[1] As a result they often place important parts of their identities—such as their family, their friends, and even their faith—in an "identity lockbox." Those important parts of themselves end up sealed away, separate from their day-to-day lives.

Demonstrate the "identity lockbox" by explaining: **I'm wearing two shirts. For many graduating seniors, faith is like my exterior shirt. It hasn't become the core of who I am. And if it hasn't become the core of who I am, I can take off my faith and put it in a lockbox.** At this point, demonstrate by taking off your shirt and putting it in your safe or suitcase.

Real Reflections from Real Students

I think what hit me right off the bat was a sense of "the fence is down" . . . the fence of your school, community, family, church, friends that was once around you. The fence of people saying "this is the type of person you are," or "this is what you are allowed and not allowed to do," or "this is what is and is not appropriate"—drops way down as soon as you get to college, and I saw that instantly. I mean, the first day on campus, your parents drive away, and no one knows you. So, suddenly, I was faced with this situation in which I could literally have re-created myself in some ways if I wanted to, and nobody would have known that I had ever been any different.

Optional: Play Part 1 of "Karis' Story" here, asking students afterward to respond to the experience Karis shares about stowing away her faith.

Ask: **How, if at all, does the identity lockbox help describe what you've seen in other high school students, college students, or adults?**

NEW

Continue: **The good news is that God intends much more for us than the identity lockbox. In fact, our relationship with God has the potential to dramatically change our identities.**

Scripture Sidebar

Throughout history many leaders and theologians have believed that the "image of God" referred to some unique quality or characteristic that's part of our human nature. These "substantive views" tend to describe God's image in us as either a physical resemblance or a spiritual quality or even our ability to reason. More recently (in theological terms, *recently* means in the last two centuries), an important additional definition of the image of God has gained support. The "relational view" suggests the image lies not in who we are or anything we possess, but in our capacity to have relationships with God and others. That means that our identities are inherently tied to our relationships with God and with each other.

At this point, distribute the **God's Vision for My Identity** handout. Go around the group, asking students to read aloud, one at a time, the names God intends for us.

Ask students to silently reread the list of identity statements on their own and take a few minutes to **draw a star** next to any of the names or phrases that have made a difference in their own lives.

Next, invite students to take a few minutes to **draw a question mark** next to any phrases that they've only somewhat experienced—or perhaps not experienced at all.

Finally, give students a few minutes to **circle** the specific names or phrases on the handout that they believe will be most important for them in the future. They won't know for sure, but they can make educated guesses.

When the labeling exercise is over, ask students if they want to share any of the terms they labeled—and why they did so. Feel free to share one or two of the identity terms that you labeled as well—and why.

NOTE: You may want to collect these handouts to mail to students during their freshman year of college, perhaps at the same time as the handout in the next section.

Optional: Play Part 2 of "Karis' Story" here, asking for students' reflections on the ways Karis' transformation and reconciliation with God stirs thoughts about how they want to live out their faith now as well as in college.

Have More Time?

Feel free to distribute paper and crayons, markers, or other art supplies to your students and have them draw images related to the identity statements that they'd like to focus on in the future. Students can take their artwork home after the session, or you can collect the artwork in order to mail to students later.

HOW

Explain: **Have you ever heard this phrase, "Begin with the end in mind"? How is that suggestion relevant as you prepare to finish high school?**

At this point, distribute the **Identity That Sticks** handout and explain that today students will take a first stab at writing a few sentences to describe who they want to be a year from now.

NOTE: Assuming you want to follow our suggestion and give students time during future sessions to modify and add to this **Identity That Sticks** handout, let students know that today is their first step toward a vision of who they want to be, and that they'll be clarifying and adding to that vision in future sessions.

Give students plenty of time to complete the handout. If you want to give students a chance to edit and expand upon their **Identity That Sticks** handout in future sessions, collect them now. If not, they can take them home.

Explain that to help "make sticky" their visions for their identities, you'll mail them their **Identity That Sticks** handouts in the future. Give each student an envelope and have them address the envelopes to themselves. (NOTE: Decide beforehand if you want their summer addresses or fall addresses; keep in mind that many of your students might not know their fall addresses yet.) Ask them to stuff their **Identity That Sticks** handouts into the envelopes and hand them back to you. (ANOTHER NOTE: Be sure they leave the envelopes unsealed as you'll be giving these back in subsequent sessions; plus you may want to include your own note later).

Next, remove the second, exterior shirt from the safe or suitcase in which you had placed it earlier, explaining that having a clear sense of who we want to be in a year and embracing these identity statements can help keep us from sealing our faith in an identity lockbox.

Collect the envelopes and place them in the

Real Reflections from Real Students

I think holding on to some of who you are can be hard in that process. So maybe write a little letter to yourself about what you regard as the most important parts of who you are and don't want to lose track of. Realize that those things might grow or change somewhat, but be aware of the parts of yourself that are important to the person you want to be always.

center of your group. Invite a few of your students to pray over the envelopes, that God would help each of you avoid locking up your faith and instead have a clear vision for who you want to be and that each of your visions would place faith in the center of all you are and do.

More Worship and Prayer

Naming

You may want to plan for time in silent prayer focused on centering our identities in Christ. Consider using the following exercise either as a guided prayer that you lead out loud (and students respond silently), or as a handout for students to use in quiet reflection.

Introduce this exercise by saying something like: **As we begin our prayer time, think for a few minutes about the importance of names.**

Names are at the core of our identities because they're the symbols we use most to identify ourselves to the world. The Bible makes a big deal about names—the name of God and names of people who follow God are really important, and often names mean specific things. In fact, on more than a few occasions in Scripture, God changes someone's name as a result of a significant encounter.

In the God's Vision for My Identity **handout we looked at some of the names Scripture gives us that call out different aspects of our identities with God. Now we're going to reflect on one of those names: Child of God.**

Distribute the **Naming** handout and invite students to read 1 John 3:1 (printed at the top of the handout) several times and then reflect on the questions.

As students seem to complete the handout, help them bring their prayer time to a close by giving them a one- or two-minute notice then voicing a closing prayer or simple "Amen." If you have time it may be helpful to debrief this prayer by asking a few questions:

What was that prayer like for you?
What kinds of images or feelings stood out during this prayer time?
What was uncomfortable for you?
What was life-giving or renewing for you?
What do you want to remember about this time with God?

GOD'S VISION FOR MY IDENTITY

Below is a list of names from Scripture that describe God's vision for your identity. Some may make you uncomfortable; some may make you laugh. Good. Take time as you're reading to hear God reveal aspects of your identity—and the church's identity—in God.

Image of God	Genesis 1:26
God's Delight	Isaiah 62:4
The Redeemed of the Lord	Isaiah 62:12
Sought Out/Desirable	Isaiah 62:12
Not Forsaken	Isaiah 62:12
Salt of the Earth	Matthew 5:13
Light of the World	Matthew 5:14, Ephesians 5:8
Beloved	John 15:9
Temple of the Holy Spirit	1 Corinthians 3:16, 6:19-20
New Creation	2 Corinthians 5:17
Chosen	1 Peter 2:9
Royal Priest	1 Peter 2:9
The Holy People/Nation	1 Peter 2:9, Isaiah 62:12
Child of God	1 John 3:1, Galatians 3:26
Bride of Christ/God	Revelation 19:7-8

IDENTITY THAT STICKS

Imagine yourself a year from now. Write down words or phrases that describe who you hope to be in the following areas . . .

In my relationship with God, I want to be . . .

In my relationship with my family, I want to be . . .

In my relationship with friends now, I want to be . . .

In my relationship with new friends, I want to be . . .

In the way I think and feel about myself, I want to be . . .

In my job or studies, I want to be . . .

Based on the words and phrases you've jotted down, write a three-to-five sentence description of who you want to be a year from now:

A year from now I want to be . . .

NAMING

> See what great love the father has lavished on us, that we should be called children of God! And that is what we are! (1 John 3:1)

What do you think it means to be God's child? How might living as a child of God shape other parts of who you are?

For a few moments, imagine God as a loving father. Whatever your own father has or hasn't been like, imagine what God as father might be like. What kinds of things does he say to you? How does he embrace you? How does he say your name?

Now imagine God "lavishing" his love on you. What kinds of images does that bring up for you? What kinds of emotions rise in you? How do you respond to that love?

Now imagine God as Father speaking these words to you before you close your prayer. Imagine him speaking your name in the appropriate places:

"See, _____ , I have engraved you on the palms of my hands." *(Isaiah 49:16)*

"_____ , you are my [child], whom I love; with you I am well pleased." *(Mark 1:11)*

3

how can i have genuine conversations with people of other faiths?

The Big Idea:

Studying your own worldview and other worldviews can help you have real dialogue with people of other faiths.

You'll Need:

Ahead of time, invite one or more college students (or recent college alums) to your meeting. The more familiar your seniors are with these collegians, the better. In addition, the more experience these college students have had dialoguing with people of other faiths, the better. Give the college students the questions listed in the **Now** section ahead of time so they can prepare, but encourage them to answer honestly without feeling like they have to be experts or give "correct" answers to the questions. Depending on the number of collegians who can attend your meeting, you can either interview them one at a time or ask them to serve together on a panel. (NOTE: If more of your graduating seniors plan to enlist in the military or enter the workforce than attend college, invite youth group graduates who are doing likewise and tailor the questions accordingly.)

A dollar bill

Pencils

Copies of **Worldview Comparison** on pages 44–45

Bibles

A few computers or laptops with Internet access. If that's not possible, print copies of Web pages that spell out different belief systems, especially those you anticipate your students will encounter in the future. They're pretty easy to find if you search online for "Islam beliefs" or "Judaism beliefs" or "agnostic beliefs," etc. (NOTE: Don't just print the first Web site you find; do a bit of searching to make sure you find one that's accurate and relatively unbiased.)

NOW

Welcome students and ask how they're doing. Then say: **One of the best ways to prepare for life after graduation is learning from those who are a few steps ahead of us.** At this point, ask the college student(s) to share their names, colleges, year in school, etc.

Continue: **To help you get ready to interact with folks who may believe differently than you do, I'm going to ask these college students a few questions.** At this point, ask the college student(s) you've invited the following questions:

What do you like, and what do you dislike, about being a college student?

How often do you have opportunities in college to interact with people of different belief systems?

Looking back upon the conversations you've had with people who believe differently, what do you think you did well, and what would you have changed if you had the chance?

If you hear something from a professor or another student that you don't believe is true, how do you go about investigating it further to determine if it's true?

Time permitting, give your seniors the chance to ask additional questions and thank the college students before you transition to the rest of the session.

Real Reflections from Real Students

A lot of the talks in youth group were kind of motivational, but they weren't as based on worldview training, and that would have been a huge plus.

NEW

Continue: **Today we're going to talk about worldviews. How would you define** *worldview*? Most simply, it's defined as our "view of the world." Another helpful way to define *worldview*: the lenses through which we make sense of what's happening around us. It is "what we believe," and how we live our lives based upon those beliefs (e.g., the choices we make, how we spend our time and money, how we interact with others, and how we determine our meaning, value, and purpose in life).

Explain: **As followers of Christ, we can't make sense of our world apart from our beliefs about God. What do you already know about God's role in the world?**

At this point, refer back to your students' big insights on the gospel from session one.

NOTE: In this session, we're inviting you and your students to more deeply explore their Christian worldview (labeled "Part A" in the forthcoming text) as well as other worldviews (labeled "Part B"). But *you* are the expert on your students and their growth areas, so feel free to emphasize Part A instead of Part B, or vice versa. You might even want to expand this content over two meetings so you can dive more deeply into both Part A and Part B.

Part A

■ Hold up a dollar bill and explain: **It's been said that the best way to identify a counterfeit dollar bill is the ability to recognize the real thing. How does that saying relate to this discussion about worldviews?**

Real Reflections from Real Students

It's a difficult journey. Before you leave your home and go into the college world, please be sure that you know what you believe. It's going to be challenged, and your faith needs to have been made strong.

Distribute pencils and copies of the **Worldview Comparison** handout to your students and ask them to complete Part A of the handout as best they can, without looking up Scriptures.

When your students are finished, ask for a volunteer to share his or her answer to the first row ("God is . . .") and then ask another volunteer(s) to look up the relevant Scripture to see what else can be added to flesh out that person's initial ideas about who God is. Work your way through all of the rows of the handout following this pattern of first hearing from a student and another student looking up Scripture.

■ When you're finished, ask: **From this exercise, where are we pretty strong and where could we use growth?**

Have More Time?

To give you kids a greater sense of historical doctrine, read the Apostles' Creed to them and give them a chance to add additional phrases to their **Worldview Comparison** handout that emerge from its verses:

I believe in God, the Father Almighty,
the Maker of heaven and earth,
and in Jesus Christ, his only Son, our Lord:
Who was conceived by the Holy Spirit,
born of the Virgin Mary,
suffered under Pontius Pilate,
was crucified, dead, and buried;
He descended into hell.
The third day he rose from the dead;
He ascended into heaven,

and sits at the right hand of God the Father Almighty;
and he will come to judge the living and the dead.
I believe in the Holy Spirit;
the holy catholic church;
the communion of saints;
the forgiveness of sins;
the resurrection of the body;
and the life everlasting.
Amen.

Part B

Continue: **In addition to understanding our own worldviews, it's also important to understand other worldviews, especially as we're getting ready to dialogue with people who believe differently than we do. President Abraham Lincoln reportedly said, "When I am getting ready to reason with a man, I spend one-third of my time thinking about myself and what I am going to say and two-thirds about him and what he is going to say." How does that relate to our conversations with people of other faiths?**

Continue: **One way to begin understanding other worldviews is to look at other belief systems. Beliefs are an important window into how worldviews are formed.** At this point, explain whatever process you've created to allow students to look at other worldviews, whether through Internet access on a few computers or Web pages you've printed prior to the meeting. If you've printed Web pages ahead of time, explain which worldviews you chose and why you chose them. If you're inviting students to do their own research as part of your meeting, let them form small groups based upon the belief system they want to explore (i.e., one handful of students looks into atheism, another group looks into Islam).

Real Reflections from Real Students

Take every opportunity to meet people you wouldn't normally meet. I've met some crazy people, but I've been able to share the gospel with them. You can plant seeds everywhere just by being who you are and asking questions. You don't need to have a big talk; it's sometimes just questions that you leave them with, and that's it. But then they may come back to you and say, "Yeah, you asked me that question, and I've thought about it since."

Point out Part B on the **Worldview Comparison** handout and ask students to answer the questions listed and jot down whatever they've learned about the worldviews they're studying.

When students have finished exploring the other worldviews, ask for volunteers to share their answers to Part B.

Ask: **If someone asked you the question, "What's so good about Christianity?" what would you say?**

HOW

Ask: **What are some stereotypes about Christians, and why do you think these stereotypes came into being?**

Continue: **Let's role-play how NOT to have a conversation about worldviews. I would love to have two of you volunteer to have a discussion about a worldview. Person #1 will play the part of someone trying to share about your beliefs. The goal of Person #2 is to interrupt Person #1 as much as possible with comments and annoying questions and to listen as little as possible.**

Have the rest of your students watch your two volunteers for a few minutes so they can vicariously experience the dynamic of one person constantly interrupting and refusing to listen. Then ask Person #1: **What was that like for you?**

Real Reflections from Real Students

There is a negative stereotype that says Christians look down on nonbelievers and are intolerant of other beliefs—mostly because of gay rights issues and mainstream discussions—so you'll have to work very hard to overcome that.

Explain: **Now let's have Person #2 try the exact opposite behaviors. Listen as intently as you can, and instead of interrupting, ask questions to help you understand what Person #1 is saying.**

Watch this conversation dynamic unfold for a few minutes and then ask Person #1: **How did it feel to be listened to?** Ask Person #2: **How did it feel to do the listening?**

Wrap up the point by explaining: **In general people won't want to hear from you until they know you've heard them. So**

40

as opposed to what we might believe, our first job isn't to explain our worldviews—it's to *listen to the other person's.*

Transition to the final point of the session by asking: **Now imagine you're in the middle of a really good conversation, and someone asks you a question about Christianity that you can't answer. (After all, there are some questions about Christianity that are hard to answer.) Can you name some of those questions that are hard to answer?** NOTE: Don't actually try to answer these questions right now, even though it may be tempting; the point is to let students voice some of the questions.

Explain: **The worst thing to do when this happens is to get defensive and argumentative. The second worst thing is to panic. Often the best thing to do when you don't know what to say is to admit it. Explain to the other person, "I do not know." But don't stop there. Make sure that you share a reason that you've decided to follow Jesus—perhaps based on an experience you've had or a story from your own life—even when you don't know all the answers. Let's practice that together.**

If you have time, divide students into pairs and give them a chance to ask each other a hard question about Christianity with the response of "I don't know, but I do know . . ." Then the students who answered the question can complete the sentence by sharing a story or two that explains why they've decided to follow Jesus, even if they don't have all the answers.

Close by giving students a chance to pray for people they already know who come from different belief systems or worldviews. Here's one way you could do that:

Read 1 Peter 3:15-16, which encourages us to be prepared to share our faith ("the reason for the hope that you have") but gives us two guidelines for doing so: use *gentleness* and *respect.* After you read the passage out loud, explain: **Unfortunately, *gentleness* and *respect* aren't words that come to mind for most nonbelievers when they think about Christians sharing their faith. Instead they**

Real Reflections from Real Students

You're probably not going to win an intellectual debate, convince anyone to just change his or her mind . . . they want to see something in you that they want, and then they're gonna ask you why you do what you do.

may describe us with words such as *obnoxious, closed-minded, militant,* or worse.

Peter gives us a different description here, and today we'll pray for people of other faiths and worldviews by using these two guidelines: gentleness and respect. When we think about the gospel message as one of love, it really makes more sense to focus on sharing from this posture.

Next set up the prayer time by inviting students to pray aloud for people of specific faiths—the ones they researched today, as well as other people they know who hold to different faiths and worldviews. Invite students to pray a few sentences, then instruct the group that after each individual prayer, everyone will repeat the following refrain:

> **May they know the hope that we have, but help us treat them with gentleness and respect.**

If that feels too long, just use the second half of the sentence. You'll probably want to write it on poster paper or project it on a screen for students as a reminder during your prayer time—or maybe even have them write it on the bottom of their **Worldview Comparison** handout as a way to remember this prayer later. Once everyone understands and is ready, begin praying. Be sure to lead the refrain yourself after the first couple of students pray, and also be sure to designate someone to close in prayer (or do so yourself) once it seems as though everyone who wants to pray aloud has done so.

> ### *Real Reflections from Real Students*
>
> College is also one of the neatest times to be bold enough to share your faith because I think the potential for impact on a college campus is enormous.

Have More Time?

A great example of a conversation about worldviews can be found in *Purple State of Mind*, a film by Craig Detweiler and John Marks. Craig and John were followers of Christ and roommates during their sophomore year of college. That year was Craig's first year in the faith—and John's last. Twenty-five years later, they reunite and have an incredibly honest conversation about what their faith meant to them in college and how they now deal with the big stuff (e.g., death, sex, the meaning of life, God, family) given their different worldviews. Several youth ministries have used this four-part video series as a highly effective conversation starter about worldviews with high school seniors. As of the printing of this book, this DVD can be purchased from Amazon for less than $20.

Have Even More Time?

Help this worldview conversation hit home by inviting students to come with you to a worship service of another religion. Be sure to find out ahead of time ways you can be particularly respectful as guests during that worship service, and whether it will even be okay for you to visit unannounced. Make sure to debrief the experience immediately after your visit by asking questions like: **What stood out to you? What was similar to our worship? What was different? What surprised you? What do you think these folks would think if they visited our worship service?**

Have Way More Time?

Of the 10 topics in this Sticky Faith curriculum, the most challenging to tackle in one session is worldviews. If you'd like a more in-depth and intellectual exploration of worldviews that encompass the difference between theism and deism, creationism, and faith and reason, you might want to check out TrueU DVD curriculum by Focus on the Family.

WORLDVIEW COMPARISON

Part A

In the columns write down how you view the world *without looking at the Scripture passages listed.* In a few minutes, you'll be able to look at the Scripture passages and add to your initial ideas.

My Worldview

God is . . . _____

Psalm 103:8-10,
1 John 4:8

Jesus is . . . _____

John 1:14, John 14:6,
Colossians 1:15-20, 1 John 4:9

People are . . . _____

Genesis 1:27, Psalm 139:14,
Matthew 9:36, Romans 3:23

The world is . . . _____

Genesis 1:1, Psalm 24: 1-2,
Isaiah 45:18, Nehemiah 9:6

Part B

Which worldview am I studying?

What did I already know about this worldview before today?

How is this worldview similar to my own?

How is it different?

What's one thing I'd like to learn more about, either through research or a conversation with someone who holds this worldview?

4

how can my faith shape
my life and career?

The Big Idea:

*Your faith is more likely to stick when it permeates your
entire life, including your future career.*

You'll Need:

Find out prices of common postgraduation items such as a Mac-
Book, a coffee blended drink, Top Ramen, Diet Coke, micro-
wave popcorn, and a large pepperoni pizza. Make sure to
include a frozen dinner and a frozen pot pie, ideally both of
which contain some of the same ingredients (i.e., chicken,
potatoes, vegetables, gravy) in your price list. If you'd like,
you can actually purchase the items and display them at your
gathering, or you can take pictures of them.

Copies of the **Faith Factor after Graduation** handout on pages
53–54

Pencils or pens

Copies of the **Jesus' Career** handout on page 55

Index cards

Bibles

Copies of students' previously completed **Identity That Sticks** handouts from session two

NOW

Welcome students and start your discussion by asking: **After you graduate from high school, what do you think you'll be buying more of?**

Divide your students into two teams (cleverly called Team 1 and Team 2 for the purposes of this explanation) and explain that you're going to play your own version of the famous TV show, *The Price Is Right.* Ask for a volunteer from Team 1 and show that volunteer a postgraduation item you priced earlier. Ask that volunteer to guess what the price is. Then give Team 2 (the opposing team) a chance to guess if the actual retail price is higher, or lower, than the guess of the Team 1 volunteer. Read the actual retail price. If Team 2 correctly guesses higher or lower, then Team 2 gets 10 points. If their guess is wrong, then Team 1 gets the 10 points.

Ask for a volunteer from Team 2 and repeat the process with a different item, this time asking Team 1 to guess whether the actual retail price is higher or lower than the guess of the Team 2 volunteer. Continue with the game, working your way through each item, making sure you display the frozen dinner and the frozen pot pie as the last two items.

Congratulate the winning team, offer a prize if you want (perhaps they can choose from among the postgraduation items you've rounded up), and then point to the frozen dinner and the frozen pot pie. Ask: **What do the frozen dinner and pot pie have in common? How are they different?**

Explain: **Too many youth group graduates who fail to stick with their faith end up viewing their lives like this frozen dinner: They view it as divided into a number of separate compartments. Their faith is one compartment, their family is another, their studies another, their friends still another.**

48

Point to the pot pie: **If a frozen-dinner faith is compartmentalized from other parts of life, Sticky Faith is more like the pot pie. In the pot pie, everything blends. Faith isn't off to the side in its own compartment. All of your life is influenced by your faith, and your faith is influenced by all of your life.**

Today we're going to talk about how we can be less like the frozen dinner and more like the pot pie.

NEW

Ask for a volunteer to read Colossians 3:17. Explain that Paul's instructions aren't that our faith only should influence what we do when we're with Christians, or at church, or when we feel like it; rather Paul wants *all* that we do—whether in word or deed—to be done as followers of the Lord Jesus.

Explain: **Today we're going to talk about how you can live out this verse after you graduate.** Distribute copies of the **Faith Factor after Graduation** handout. Feel free to either have students write down their answers or use the questions on the handout to launch a group discussion. Either way, encourage students to move beyond vague answers like "I can pray for others" or "I can be nice to others." Those are both true, but your students can probably come up with more specific ideas.

Debrief the exercise by asking: **Which situations on the sheet are easiest for you to view from a faith perspective, and which are the hardest? Why do you think that is?**

Then ask: **What surprised you or caused you to think about your life or your faith in a different way?**

HOW

Continue: **Now that we've looked at how your faith can touch different parts of your life, we're going to take some time to think**

Real Reflections from Real Students

If anyone, especially a student, is going into college saying, "I want to know how best to honor God in my situation that I'm going into," then that person can succeed. I don't think that anyone who goes through life looking for opportunities to honor God will be left hanging or not know what to do.

Scripture Sidebar

The questions that others asked about Jesus show just how "ordinary" and "lowly" they perceived him to be. Not only did the people ask a question about Jesus' career, but they also asked, "Isn't this Mary's son?" It was not customary among Jews to describe a man as the son of his mother, so by asking if Jesus was Mary's son, they were degrading Jesus' standing.

together about how your faith can influence one area important to most of you as graduating seniors: your future career. Let's start by thinking about a career that doesn't seem like it has much to do with faith: a sofa maker. What would a sofa maker do who wanted to live his faith like the pot pie? What would he not do?

Odds are good that your students won't have a lot of specific ideas for a furniture maker, and that's okay. Affirm what they do share and then ask for a volunteer to read Matthew 13:55. Explain: **Jesus' dad, Joseph, was a carpenter.**

Next ask a student to read Mark 6:3 aloud. Then continue: **Not only was Jesus' dad a carpenter, Jesus himself was most likely trained as a carpenter. Sophisticated carpentry and furniture-making tools of today didn't exist in the first century. As a result, Jesus did a lot of heavy lifting—literally. Unlike how Jesus is often portrayed, as a carpenter, Jesus would have been no wimp.**

Distribute pencils and copies of **Jesus' Career** to your students, asking them to complete the handout. When they've finished, walk through the questions with them, inviting them to share their answers.

Ask: **Sometimes it seems like the only way your faith can really influence your career is if you become a pastor or a missionary. What do we learn from reflecting upon Jesus as a carpenter?**

If you have time, distribute copies of the *Identity That Sticks* handout that students first completed in session two. Give students a few minutes to edit and expand their descriptions of themselves at the bottom of the handout in regard to how they want their faith to influence their lives and career choices. Invite a few volunteers to share any changes or additions they've made to their visions of themselves a year from now.

Have More Time?

Help your students continue to think about how their faith can influence their lives, as well as others' lives, by inviting them to anonymously write down the careers they plan to pursue on index cards. If they don't know yet, have them write down an outlandish career (i.e., trapeze artist, rodeo clown). Collect the index cards and read the careers one at a time, giving students a chance to brainstorm how their faith could influence their pursuit of that career. Have fun with some of the more outlandish career ideas, seeing what zany options your students come up with.

To close the discussion, invite students to share prayer requests, especially those that relate to ways they want their faith to make a difference in their lives—either now or in the future. After each student shares, ask for a volunteer who will pray aloud for that particular request. After all the requests have been shared, close in prayer, inviting those who said they would pray aloud to do so.

More Worship and Prayer

If it's not already a familiar practice in your group, introduce students to what's been historically known as the *Jesus Prayer*, a simple one-line phrase repeated over and over:

Today we're going to learn a really simple prayer practice that's been around since at least the sixth century A.D. The words are:

"Lord Jesus Christ, Son of God, have mercy on me, a sinner."

Or a shorter version if you'd rather:

"Lord Jesus Christ, have mercy on me," or even just
"Lord Jesus, have mercy."

The way many people pray this prayer is to say the words over and over again, letting them be reminders to point their hearts toward Jesus' mercy—meaning his love and grace. Sometimes when we're not sure what else to pray, the Jesus Prayer can be a simple way of reminding us of the power of Jesus' love and grace in our lives. In fact, it's also called

51

Prayer of the Heart, perhaps because it's a simple and powerful prayer to repeat quietly in our hearts throughout our days.

So we're going to take time to pray this prayer silently as we close this session. But I'm going to invite you to pray it actively—moving around. Since our focus today has been on taking Jesus with us into every area of our lives, let's get up and walk around as we pray. (NOTE: You'll want to give students some parameters based on the time allotted and your location. Ideally students could leave the room so they're not awkwardly running across each other's paths. If they can easily get outdoors to walk around, all the better.) **As you walk and pray, notice the rhythms that develop. Walk your footsteps to the beat of the prayer, or breathe in and out to the pace of the words.**

Feel free to adapt it as a prayer for others. For example, instead of saying "on me" say "on this neighborhood," "on our church," "on the people I'll meet at college," or wherever else you'd like to invite God's mercy and grace to flow.

Instruct students if and where you'll meet back to close your time. Remind them of the words of the prayer again, then set them loose.

If you can create space and have time to debrief the prayer exercise, ask questions like:

What was it like to pray this prayer today?
What particular thoughts or emotions did it raise for you?
Could you see yourself using this prayer as a guide more often? Why or why not?
How do you think this prayer could help you integrate your faith into your work, your play, and other parts of everyday life?

FAITH FACTOR AFTER GRADUATION

And whatever you do, whether in word or deed, do it all in the name
of the Lord Jesus, giving thanks to God the Father through him.

Colossians 3:17

After graduation, how can your faith influence you and others around you when you are:
Driving (and running late)?

Showing up to class for the first time (and nervous about all the new homework)?

Showing up to a new job (and wondering how to relate to your coworkers)?

Showing up to an old job (that you don't like)?

Studying for finals (and doing some last-minute cramming)?

Texting or posting an online update (when you're feeling down)?

Texting or posting an online update (when you're feeling great)?

Working out (in a new gym where everyone is checking out each other)?

Hearing your alarm clock (and wondering if anyone will really care if you skip your class this morning)?

Going to a party (and you're not sure if you're going to drink)?

Working at the nearby coffee house (when the customer who annoys you walks in)?

Hearing about a ministry need at your church (and wondering if God might want you to respond)?

JESUS' CAREER

So if Jesus was a carpenter, how would he have let his faith influence . . .
His work schedule?

The quality of his work?

His relationships with his coworkers?

His response to a dissatisfied customer (as if Jesus ever created flawed furniture!)?

His response to someone who was late making a payment?

His response to someone who was trying to take advantage of him?

The way he handled business finance and managed the accounting books?

5

how can my struggles help my faith stick?

The Big Idea:

Problems, crises, and doubts don't have to deal a death blow to our faith; in fact, they can help us move forward on our faith journeys.

You'll Need:

Sticky notes—enough for each student to have at least four

Copies of the **My Lament** handout on page 67

Pens/pencils

Optional: Drawing supplies for students to use if they want to draw on the back of their **My Lament** handout

Ahead of time: Contact some of your former youth group students who are now in college and ask them to send you a quick response to the following question: **What are one or two questions, struggles, or doubts you or other Christians you know have had since starting college?** They can answer via email, text, or whatever media works best (even better if they can send short video responses you can show your students on a phone or computer). Be sure to let them know that you're going to share their answers with current seniors, and ask if they'd prefer to remain anonymous.

A Magic 8 Ball. You can use a real Magic 8 Ball for this, or you can use an electronic version: a quick online search for "Magic 8 Ball" will return several browser-based interactive 8 balls, and smart phone 8 ball apps are plentiful.

Optional: If you decide to watch the video "What You Need to Know about Faith in College" on the DVD, be sure to figure out ahead of time how you'll show the video (laptop, projector, etc.) and set up accordingly. Alternatively you could send students a link to the video later to watch as a follow-up to the session.

NOW

Welcome students and hand out two sticky notes to each of them, asking them to take a few moments to think about one "high" and one "low" from the last week—something that was life-giving and something that was life-draining. Invite them each to write their high on one sticky note and their low on the other.

Then invite each student to share out loud their high and stick it on a wall somewhere high up; then do the same with their low except stick it—you guessed it—somewhere low. (NOTE: This introductory exercise is actually really important to the rest of the session, so please don't skip it!)

Next ask: **Do you agree or disagree with this statement:** *Most Christian students have doubts about their faith*? Ask those who agree to raise their hands, then those who disagree. Invite a few students to share why they believe it's true, then invite a few more to share their reasons for disagreeing. Refrain from adding your opinion to this discussion, and when appropriate ask the next question:

Do you agree or disagree with this statement: *God doesn't want us to doubt our faith?*

Again, ask for all those who agree to raise their hands, then those who disagree; allow one or two students to share their reasons for choosing each position.

Continue: **Research has actually shown that *most* students—about 70 percent—doubt their faith in high school, but fewer than half actually *talk about* those doubts with a youth pastor, other adult, or other students in their youth ministry.**[1]

Ask: **Why do you suppose fewer than half of students who doubt their faith in high school talk to anyone about those doubts?**

Ask: **Now think ahead to next year: What kinds of questions or struggles do you guess might come up in college?**

After students share some ideas, let them know you've asked some of their youth group friends who've gone on to college to share one or two questions, struggles, or doubts they've had since starting college. Then read some of the responses you received (or show the videos).

Now lighten up the conversation just a bit by saying something like: **Many of us tend to handle these good—and really important—questions a bit like this toy we might have played with when we were kids.** Pull out your Magic 8 Ball (or your laptop or smart phone version) and ask students to suggest questions for the Magic 8 Ball. After a couple of rounds, transition to this discussion:

Now think about the questions, doubts, and problems you have for God—the ones we brought up or others we didn't. How is coming to God with those questions different from coming to the Magic 8 Ball?

Real Reflections from Real Students

Entering my sophomore year of college, I became very disappointed with life. I had all these ideas about college, and it wasn't necessarily going how I wanted. I was feeling very far away from God and very dry spiritually, struggling to find a church and a church family where I could fit in at school. And as I went through that long struggle, basically spiritual darkness . . . when I came out of it I found God waiting for me on the other side, and realized that he'd been with me through that struggle, through that time of questioning and doubts and searching.

59

When the Fuller Youth Institute asked college students to reflect on their doubts in high school, they wondered:

If God would still love me if I had sex. Most of my doubts circulated around sex actually.

I would doubt if I was worth anything.

If God really existed.

If God would forgive me for all the bad things I had done and was doing.

Why God would allow terrible things to happen if he was so loving and sensitive.

Why do I feel like I am never able to hear God?

Homosexuality—is it really such a bad thing?

Do non-Christians really go to hell, even if they are good people?

Say: **Unfortunately, the way we throw out a question and shake the Magic 8 Ball is sometimes all-too-similar to the way we approach our real questions and doubts: We don't realize that the God of the universe is happy to talk about that stuff. God actually wants us to ask hard questions. God can handle them.**

NEW

Continue: **Here's some good news: Doubts and struggles can form our faith in stronger and perhaps more lasting ways than when we don't experience doubts and struggles. In fact, some studies have shown that those who face their questions and doubts (rather than pushing them down or pretending they don't exist) emerge with stronger faith in the end.[2]**

Similarly, crises are often what stretch our faith the most. Let's be honest: No one wants to experience a crisis. But as life happens to us, we find ourselves face-to-face with ugly stuff. Your parents divorce. A friend is killed in a car accident. Your little sister gets pregnant. These things can launch us into new layers of questions and doubts, prompting us to ask, "Where is God?" Even though we typically try to avoid pain, most real growth in our lives requires pain of some kind.

If you have an appropriate story to share from a crisis experience that shook your faith, now is a good time to share that with students. Focus on the ways the experience stretched you and caused you to ask questions you'd never asked before—or caused you to encounter God in new ways in the midst of the process. But be careful not to wrap it in too neat a package—the point of this example is to help students realize that facing hard stuff

60

will inevitably lead to new questions in their faith. Then transition to the following discussion, which is the heart of this NEW section.

While Scripture is no Magic 8 Ball to give us answers to all our questions, the Bible does have an interesting and kind of surprising place where doubts and struggles are freely expressed: It's called the book of Psalms.

The writers of the Hebrew songs and prayers that became the worship book of God's people were not afraid to boldly ask God to show up in the midst of ugly stuff. Of the 150 psalms, more than a third—65 actually—are considered laments.[3]

Ask: **What is a *lament*? How would you describe a lament, or the act of lamenting?** One basic definition of lament is "a cry out to God." It's both an act of grief and of asking for help. In fact, lament is usually something we do in the dark places—often the darkest points of our life journeys. For example, Psalm 88 ends with the phrase, "darkness is my closest friend" (v. 18).

Continue: **One of the most frequently asked questions in Scripture is "How long, oh Lord?" It's an important question because it calls God to do something to end our pain or others' pain. Let's look at Psalm 13 as an example.**

Have students find Psalm 13 in their Bibles so they can follow along. Divide the verses between several volunteer student readers (if you have at least six students, assign each verse to separate readers). Then ask:

Real Reflections from Real Students

My relationship with God since leaving high school has been a roller coaster. At first it may sound like a negative thing, but it isn't necessarily. We all need those little dips in order to bring ourselves to a higher understanding of God's glory and power . . . The post-high school roller coaster . . . was a chance to see God in new ways.

Real Reflections from Real Students

I've had more life experiences over the last four years, and I've been in more difficult situations and been faced with more challenges. I think that has definitely solidified my faith. I've had to ask more difficult questions, which at first made my faith rocky—but once I worked through those questions, my faith become more solid; it's definitely grown stronger than it was years ago or weeks ago.

Scripture Sidebar

You may want to weave some of these points into your discussion of Psalm 13.

Psalm 13 is considered an individual lament, but there are also corporate laments that the community might pray or sing together.

Like many psalms of lament, this one begins with a desperate cry "How long," includes a prayer for deliverance, and takes a sharp turn in verse 5 to conclude on a tone of trust in God's faithful covenant love.

The "enemy" referred to in verses 2 and 4 could be a person or an illness, but many commentators believe the enemy is a reference to death itself. The prayer for God to "Give light to my eyes" is for restoration of health and relief from grieving, but also a counterpart to the feeling of God hiding his face (verse 1). If God would "Look!" (verse 3), this worshiper would be restored to God's presence and healed from impending death.

What are some words or images that describe what we just read? How do you feel about talking to God this way?

Ask: **How is the psalmist's prayer in verse 5 different from saying, "Oh, it'll be okay," or "I'm fine"?** You may want to note here that often—but not always—a psalm of lament ends with an expression of hope that things will change, that God will respond, and that the person praying this prayer still trusts God as good.

Ask: **Verse 5 uses the word** *trust* **for the first time in the psalm—"But I trust in your unfailing love." What does trusting God in tough times have to do with developing Sticky Faith?**

At this point, refer back to your students' big insights on the gospel from session one. You might want to remind students that just as Jesus is bigger than our mistakes, he's also bigger than our doubts.

Say: **Laments like this don't answer all our questions, but lamenting can be a helpful part of strengthening our faith by reminding us that** *answers aren't everything.* **As the psalmists proclaim over and over, the "unfailing love" of God isn't wiped out by anything: not our crises, not our doubts, and not even our sins.**

HOW

> Optional: Play the "What You Need to Know about Faith in College" video as a transition to the HOW section, soliciting students' thoughts about how these youth workers' words raise new questions or responses in them.

Continue: **The good news is that when we face struggles—now or down the road in college—we're free to come to God with the same kind of honesty the person who wrote Psalm 13 expressed. In fact, we're going to practice doing it today.**

Distribute copies of the **My Lament** handout and pens, and read aloud the instructions at the top. Be sure to pause and ask if there are any questions, reiterating that there really is no wrong way to write a prayer of lament. In fact, if students would rather, they can turn the handout over and draw a picture instead of (or in addition to) writing words on the front. Be sure to give ample time for students to work on this prayer and encourage them to spread out to help them feel more alone with God.

When you call students back together, be sure to allow some time to debrief this process before moving on. Some may have finished this exercise with very little emotional connection, but others may have been uncomfortable or experienced disturbing feelings. Be prepared to be at your pastoral "best" and navigate sharing that could become unhelpful or inappropriate. You may need to invite some students to stay after or set up times to meet privately if they need to process more outside the group.

The following are some debrief questions you could use, depending on your time and students' level of engagement:

Real Reflections from Real Students

I think one thing I would want high school seniors to know is that they'll face difficult questions that might rock their faith, and I would emphasize how important it is that they continue to read the word of God and put themselves among bodies of believers, planting themselves among believers and getting encouraged—and especially getting fed spiritually by more mature believers.

You don't have to share the content of what you were lamenting, but would anyone like to share how it felt to pray this way?

How do you suppose it might change your relationship with God to pray these kinds of prayers? How do you think it could change our relationships with each other if we prayed together this way sometimes? If no one answers, you might offer a reminder that sharing our struggles with each other is part of what it means to be on a journey of faith together as brothers and sisters in Christ. Grieving and hurting together can strengthen both our faith and our friendships.

Ask: **Remember how we started today's session?** Give students a minute to think about it before helping them out (by sharing "highs and lows" from the week). **What do you suppose is the value of sharing your high and low experiences with others?**

Continue: **Now think ahead to what life may be like next year. What do you suppose may be some of the highs and lows of your first few months of college?**

Again, distribute two sticky notes for each student, explaining that they should write on one what they anticipate will be a high after they graduate and, on the other, what they believe may be a low. Give students some time to write on each sticky note, and if you want you can let them use more sticky notes for more ideas. Like before, instruct students to stick their "highs" high on the walls around the room and their "lows" in low spots—except this time they'll post them without sharing the highs or lows out loud.

After everyone has contributed potential highs and lows to the walls, invite students to walk around the room and look at how their peers are anticipating both the joys and laments of the first few months of college. Then gather everyone together in a circle and ask for a few volunteers to pray that all of you would sense God's presence in both the highs and the lows of life beyond high school, and that no one would face those highs and lows alone.

More Worship and Prayer

If you have more time to incorporate creative worship into your session, consider setting up the following worship experience. Ahead of time, or as you explain the process, find an open space in your meeting spot to either lay a cross on the floor and set up tea light candles along its length and width, or set up candles on the floor in the shape of a cross. Then introduce the experience as follows:

Scripture encourages us that the presence of God is not the only place we can express our tough stuff, but the presence of other believers is also an appropriate context in which to share and be supported in our struggles.

We've probably all heard about "Doubting Thomas"—the disciple who missed out on the first post-resurrection appearance of Jesus to his disciples and then had trouble believing it was true (John 20:24-29). Let's be honest: Plenty of us would likely have had the same response; no "doubt" it was more than a little strange!

What's remarkable about Jesus' response to Thomas at his next appearance is that he allows Thomas to question in the presence of his fellow disciples and of Jesus himself. Then he leads Thomas to a place of new trust, inviting him to touch Jesus' resurrected body.

Just as Thomas could doubt out loud with other believers and with Jesus himself, our reflections on our high points AND our low points—even our struggles, doubts, and failures—can be an important part of our faith journey.

Next light one candle at the center of the cross, and one at each end of the horizontal bar, telling students they represent the wounds at Jesus' hands and side. Enter into a time of worship through singing or playing instrumental music, and invite students during that time to approach the cross and each take an unlit candle and light it from one of the flames representing Jesus' wounds, setting it back on the cross where they each picked it up. Let this be an act of worship that represents coming to Jesus with our doubts and hearing him invite us to touch his wounds and trust him to be real in the midst of our struggles.

As you set this up, invite students to speak a doubt or question to God *out loud* as they light their candles. Say, **Following Thomas' example, we're giving each other permission to speak our struggles aloud in the presence of Christ and other believers.** *However, if you believe the safety and/or maturity level of your group won't handle this well, don't include the "out loud" part in the instructions.* When it's time to close, pray something along these lines: **Just as we lit our candles in the presence of Christ and of each other, may we grow in our faith as we share our struggles in the presence of Christ and of other believers, both now and next year beyond high school.**

MY LAMENT

A lament is a cry out to God in grief, pain, suffering, or repentance, believing that God hears us and takes us seriously. Often a lament ends in hope—remembering that God is faithful and good and compassionate.

You may or may not have ever prayed this way before, but this exercise will give you an opportunity to experience coming to God with your doubts, struggles, and pain. *There is no wrong way to do it.* Further down are some open-ended prompts to get you started, but if they're not useful to you, skip them. Similarly, this handout ends with some words from Psalm 130, but feel free to add your own ending instead.

Oh Lord, how long . . . ?
Sometimes I wonder if . . .

God, are you really . . . ?

I don't understand why . . .

It hurts me when I think about . . .

God, I wish you would show up when . . .

Out of the depths we cry to you, Lord;
Lord, hear our voices.
Let your ears be attentive to our cry for mercy.
I wait for the Lord, my whole being waits,
And in his word I put my hope.

Psalm 130:1-2, 5

6

how can my friends help my faith stick?

The Big Idea:

Your faith and friendships will grow as you ask each other hard—but important—questions.

You'll Need:

Two student helpers. Ahead of time, ask a male student to read the part of Samson in Judges 16:4-22 and a female student to read the part of Delilah. You, or another student, can read everything else.

Bibles

Index cards

Pens or pencils

Copies of the **A Little Help from My Friends** handout on page 76

Copies of students' previously completed **Identity That Sticks** handouts from session two

Optional: If you decide to watch the video "What You Need to Know about Life After Youth Group" on the DVD, be sure to figure out ahead of time how you'll show the video (laptop, projector, etc.) and set up accordingly. Alternatively you could send students a link to the video later to watch as a follow-up to the session.

NOW

Welcome students and check in to see how they're doing. Explain: **I'm going to read six statements about friends. After I read each statement, I'll say, "Go," and then you'll each move to the part of the room that most closely reflects where you stand on each statement. The left side of the room is for those who disagree completely; the middle of the room means you're not sure where you stand, or you'd rather not say; the right side of the room is for those who agree completely.**

Read the first statement: **If you become just like your friends, you're selling out to your true self**. Give students a few seconds to find the place in the room that best reflects their opinions. After students have found places to stand, invite them to find a partner standing near them and each pair explain to each other why they chose that part of the room. Then ask a few volunteers to explain to the group why they're standing where they are.

Repeat the process with each of the remaining statements:

Who you become depends on who you're hanging out with.
Your closest friends should be the same gender as you.
Your closest friends should be as committed to their faith as you.
The more you share your secrets with a friend, the greater the risk to you.
If you see a friend making a mistake, you should talk to him or her about it as soon as possible.

After you finish reading the final statement about the friend making a mistake, ask:

70

Would your answer change if I told you your friend's mistake was HUGE? What if it was a pretty minor mistake?

NEW

Explain: **We're going to look at a Bible story that might be familiar to many of you, but today we're going to see it through new "Sticky Faith" lenses. One of the more unusual people in the Bible was a man named Samson.**

Samson's superhuman strength came from something called a "Nazirite vow," which meant his strength depended on maintaining a certain lifestyle (see Judges 13:7 and 16:17).

But Samson had one big problem: He made unwise choices when it came to women. The Philistines were bitter enemies of Israel, but in Judges 14, Samson almost married a Philistine woman.

Let's turn to Judges 16 to read more about Samson's problems with women.

Distribute Bibles and read Judges 16:4-22 with your two student helpers. You're likely to hear some chuckling if your Judges 16:7 translation refers to "thongs" instead of "bowstrings"—it's best to quickly explain that "thongs" are a type of reed.

Skip ahead to Judges 16:23-31 and invite another volunteer to read what ends up happening to Samson.

Ask: **Girls, how would you describe Delilah in this passage?**

Ask: **Guys, how would you describe Samson?**

Ask: **Why do you suppose Samson eventually told the truth about his Nazirite vow?**

Continue: **You might be wondering how this passage relates to Sticky Faith or friendship. Well, Samson's life would have been a whole**

Scripture Sidebar

The Philistines are believed to be an uncircumcised people who descended from Ham, Noah's son. They worshiped two Babylonian gods: Dagon and Ashtaroth. By the time of Samson, they had been oppressors of Israel for 40 years (Judges 13:1).

lot different if he had some good friends who could have intervened in this mess with Delilah. After all, Delilah tricked him three times. Where were his good friends who could have said to him, "Samson, your girlfriend is acting funky"? Where were his buddies who could have reminded him that love doesn't just make us blind—that sometimes it makes us stupid, too?

Ask: **What keeps us from talking to our friends when we see them making mistakes?** Odds are good that your students will answer with "I don't want to interfere," "I don't want to seem like a know-it-all or a goodie-goodie," and "I don't want to lose the friendship."

That's a good setup for one of the main points of the session. Continue: **These are understandable obstacles, but there's one strategy that can overcome all of these obstacles. What if, instead of assuming we have to correct or lecture our friends, we choose to ask them questions instead?**

Ask: **What's the difference between asking questions and giving a lecture?**

At this point share an example from your own life of the power of a friend asking you the right question(s). If you don't have an example from your own life, make one up. (Just kidding. Don't do that. Just skip ahead to the next part of the discussion.)

Distribute index cards and pencils and give your students a few minutes to write down a few sentences that describe a struggling friend. Explain that you'll be reading these cards aloud to the group, so they can go as deep as they are comfortable, but they shouldn't share anything that reveals the friend's identity.

Real Reflections from Real Students

The relationships I've had with youth group or with a faith community have been generally a lot deeper where we're trying to understand each other and really keeping each other accountable and checking up on each other.

Collect the index cards and explain: **I will choose an index card and read the friend's struggle, and I'd like us to discuss together the types of questions that might be helpful to ask this friend. Keep in mind that good questions are open ended, meaning they can't be answered by just a "yes" or "no."**

Discuss as many cards as your time allows. With each new index card, see if students can figure out how to bring up the topic in a way that's natural and not too awkward. For example, if a student wants to talk to a friend about her partying, she could ask, "Hey, can I ask you a question? How are you feeling about your partying?" or "Can we talk about your partying?"

After students have thought about how to bring up the challenging subjects mentioned on the index cards, encourage them to come up with next-step questions. If students get stuck, you might give the following examples of good questions:

What are some options you can think of?
What adult can you talk to about what you're experiencing?
What are you gaining by what you're doing?
What is it costing you?
What would you say to someone else who was in your situation?

HOW

Explain: **Recently high school seniors in youth groups around the country were asked what they wanted more of in their youth groups; the top answer was time for deep conversation.[1] Accountability—which means the type of relationships in which we can ask each other hard and important questions—came in fourth.**

Students are likely to want to know what else seniors wanted more of from their youth groups. If they're curious, the following are the results of the survey:

What do you want to see more of in youth group?[2]

Rank	Item	Rank	Item
1	Time for deep conversation	8	Bible study
2	Mission trips	9	Small groups
3	Service projects	10	Camps
4	Accountability	11	Time for questions
5	One-on-one time with leaders	12	Student leadership
6	Retreats	13	Games
7	Time for worship		

> Optional: At this point you may want to play the "What You Need to Know about Life after Youth Group" video. Ask students how these youth workers' reflections about friendships in college stir new thoughts or questions for them.

Distribute copies of the **A Little Help from My Friends** handout and give students several minutes to think of one or two questions in each category. To get the ball rolling, you might want to pick one of the categories and discuss together the types of questions that might help students make better decisions and have more Sticky Faith. For example, for "family," good questions might include: *What have you done lately to show your parents that you're thinking about them? How will you connect with your parents when you see them this weekend? How can you pray for your parents? How would you like your parents to pray for you?*

When students have completed their handouts, ask for volunteers to share the questions they felt would be helpful in each category.

If it feels appropriate, emphasize that the goal of these questions isn't to create some sort of "religious behavior" quiz or to judge each other. Instead the goal is to support each other in a spirit of grace and mercy, not condemnation or judgment.

Explain: **At the bottom of this handout write down the name of a friend who you want to ask you some of the questions you've just developed. Even if you drift a bit from this person after graduation, if you're able to write down his or her name now, odds are good that you could still call him or her after graduation and share what's going on in your life.**

It's quite possible that some students won't think of friends who they'd feel comfortable discussing these sorts of questions. To help those students without embarrassing them or pointing them out, ask the entire group: **If some of us can't think of someone with whom we'd feel comfortable discussing these questions, what can we do?**

Depending on the closeness of relationships in the group, it's also quite possible that some students will have identified someone in the room as a friend they'd consider asking for help with accountability. Encourage students to get with that person—whether in the room or not—after your meeting or sometime this week to follow up on creating the kind of relationship where questions can be safely asked and answered.

Have More Time?

Gather your group in a circle and explain: **Already in this youth group, we've seen God use others to build up our faith. I'm wondering if a few of you would share how others in this circle have asked you questions, or prayed with you, or have been there for you when you were struggling, or have in other ways been good examples of Sticky Faith.** Give your students plenty of time to share. (NOTE: You and other adult leaders should keep eyes out for students who aren't being mentioned by others around the circle so you can highlight ways that they have somehow impacted you so they don't feel left out.)

If you have time, distribute copies of the *Identity That Sticks* handout that students completed in session two. Give students a few minutes to edit and expand their descriptions of themselves at the bottom of the handouts in regard to the types of friendships they'd like to strengthen or develop in the next year. Invite a few volunteers to share changes/ additions to their visions of themselves a year from now.

Close in prayer, thanking God for how God's already worked through your friendships and asking God to help you go deeper with each other—and new friends—as you move into this new chapter.

A LITTLE HELP FROM MY FRIENDS

As you're preparing for next year, list one or two questions for each category below that a friend could ask you that might help you make better decisions and have more Sticky Faith.

Questions about your . . .

Relationship with God

Friends and roommates

Romantic relationship(s)

Family

Partying habits (or lack thereof)

Use of your time

Studies

Job

7

how will i respond to the party scene in college?

The Big Idea:

I can make Sticky Faith choices about partying that fit who I want to be in college.

You'll Need:

To consider convening this meeting at a college or university, preferably at night, and preferably not a Christian college. The goal is to get students thinking about the party scene at college—and that will be a bit easier at night and at a secular school. Your ideal meeting space on that campus is one that's somewhat private and allows for a good conversation but is close to some of the student hubs on campus (e.g., a lounge or corner of a student center).

To show up at the college at least 60 minutes before your students and walk around to see where signs of the "party scene" are most obvious (e.g., flyers advertising parties, beer bottles, loud music).

To make sure you have enough adult supervision for small groups of students to go on a 15-to-30 minute campus walk. Ahead of time, you might want to prep the adults about what you're hoping happens on the walk (i.e., it's not a time to pass judgment but rather to observe).

Copies of the **Party Trends in College** handout on page 85

Bibles

Copies of students' **Identity That Sticks** handout from session two

Pencils

Copies of the **Fit or Fight?** handout on page 86–87

Pillows you've placed in two different places of your meeting spaces that students can use to kneel upon

A way to display 1 John 1:9 for each student, whether on paper you've printed ahead of time or writing the text of the verse on a whiteboard or poster paper

Optional: If you decide to watch the video "The Jacket" found on the accompanying DVD, be sure to figure out ahead of time how you'll show the video (laptop, projector, etc.) and set up accordingly. Alternatively you could send students a link to the video later to watch as a follow up-to the session.

NOTE: If it's not feasible for you to meet at a college campus, feel free to simply begin your discussion with your students after the note on page 79.

NOW

Greet students and ask them to look around where you're meeting. Explain: **Anytime we're in a new space, we can actually tell a lot about it just by looking around. Ask: Setting aside what you may already know about this school, what can you immediately learn about this college just by looking around?**

To help prompt students to observe their surroundings more carefully, ask: **What do you see? What do you smell? What do you hear?**

We'll divide up into groups of two to three each, and then an adult leader will go with each group on a brief walk around this campus, seeing what you can learn—not just about the school overall but more specifically about the party scene. At this point repeat the questions in the previous paragraph to help students stay attuned to what they see, hear, etc. Based on what you observed when you showed up to the campus early, point groups toward areas that are more likely to have signs of partying. Let your students and adults know that the goal isn't to pass judgment or gawk at college students, but rather to walk around and observe. Agree upon a time to return to your meeting space.

When students return, ask: **What did you see?**

Ask: **What did you smell?**

Ask: **What did you hear?**

Ask: **What surprised you?**

Ask: **What confirmed what you expected?**

Ask: **If you didn't notice many signs of the party scene, why do you think that is?**

NOTE: If it's not feasible for you to meet at a college campus, feel free to simply begin your discussion with your students after this point.

Ask: **In general, what have you heard about the post-high school party scene?**

Ask: **How is it similar or different to parties in high school?**

Ask: **What have you heard about sex in college?**

Ask: **How about alcohol and drugs?**

Real Reflections from Real Students

I would tell high school seniors to prepare, to plan ahead. When you go away to college, you don't just say "I'm going to leave, I want to go here," and just pack your bags and go. You learn about it, you find out what the environment is going to be like, if you're going to need furniture in your dorm, and what kind of clothes you're going to need to prepare for the weather. If you're going to do that amount of preparing for moving, your faith needs the same kind of preparation. Look into what the college environment can provide for you positively, and maybe expose you to negatively, and prepare for all of that. Know your faith and be willing and strong enough to let it be challenged.

Explain: **While the party scene is different at every school, the following trends have emerged among high school graduates attending colleges around the country.**[1] Distribute the **Party Trends in College** handout to students and review it together.

> *Having a moral "to do" (or perhaps more accurately, a "not to do") list doesn't cut it.* There are so many new temptations and choices in college, you can't rely on lists. You need a more robust process to help you make wise decisions.
>
> *Who you hang out with in college makes a huge difference.* Many students find that if their best friends party, they do also. If you end up with friends who don't party at all or don't party as much, you'll be less likely to party.
>
> *Many college freshmen party primarily because they want to make friends.* If you're a new college student feeling lonely, you're more likely to look to parties as a way to meet people and make friends.
>
> *Once students start to party, they feel "locked in" to partying.* Your choices in the first week or two tend to set you on a path that's pretty hard to step away from.
>
> *It's not "if" you'll have the opportunity to party and have sex and drink alcohol, but "when."* Partying is so rampant for college students and young adults that we need to have authentic, honest conversations about it now.

Emphasize that you're hoping today you'll have an honest dialogue about partying—one that moves away from "Sunday school" answers and gets real about the types of choices your students will face in a few months.

NEW

Distribute students' **Identity That Sticks** handouts from session two. (NOTE: If students have not yet completed this exercise, make sure you build an extra 15 minutes into this session and distribute copies of pages 32–33 and invite your students to dream about who they want to be in college by completing the **Identity That Sticks** handout.)

Give students a minute or two to silently reread the identity they have previously developed and explain: **Today we're going to see how identity plays itself out in the midst of sex, drugs, and alcohol.**

Distribute Bibles and invite students to turn to 1 Corinthians 6:12-20. Ask for student volunteer(s) to read the verses and then work your way verse by verse using the following questions and discussion prompts.

Verse 12: Paul is quoting some of the Corinthians who thought they "have the right to do anything."

Verse 13: Paul quotes the Corinthians again by saying, "Food for the stomach and the stomach for food, and God will destroy them both." This quotation shows the Corinthian belief that our physical bodies, and what we put into our bodies (i.e., food), are both temporary. God will destroy them both, so therefore we can do whatever we want with our bodies, and eat whatever we want as well.

When Paul writes, "The body, however, is not meant for sexual immorality but for the Lord, and the Lord for the body," what do you suppose Paul is trying to say?

Verse 14: What happened to Jesus' body? What will happen to our bodies? How is that relevant to what Paul wrote in verse 13?

Verse 15: Paul uses a pretty vivid image here of Jesus being united with a prostitute. How is that relevant to what seems to be Paul's main point thus far?

Verses 16-17: What happens to someone who has sex with a prostitute? While it's not mentioned in this verse, what do you think happens to those who have sex with those who aren't prostitutes but aren't their spouses, either?

Verse 18: The Greek verb tense for Paul's command to "flee" suggests that one is to flee from sin *continually*. Why do you suppose Paul uses that verb tense?

Verses 19-20: When you hear the phrase "temple of the Holy Spirit," what do you think of?

Ask: **What does Paul mean when he says, "You are not your own, for you were bought at a price"?**

Scripture Sidebar

The city of Corinth was well known in the first century for its open immorality. Worshipers of Aphrodite, the goddess of love, practiced prostitution in the name of religion. At one time 1,000 sacred priestesses (prostitutes) served Aphrodite at her temple. The debauchery at Corinth was so well known that the Greek verb "to Corinthianize" came to mean "to practice sexual immorality."

Refocus students' attention on verse 12 by asking for a student volunteer to read the verse. Then explain: **Paul gives us two important questions to ask as we think about our choices, including our choices about sex and alcohol:** *First, is it beneficial? Second, will it master me?*

One way to think about these questions in the midst of the identities you've outlined on your handout is to ask more simply: *Does this choice fit who I want to be, or does it fight against who I want to be?*

Distribute copies of the **Fit or Fight?** handout and pencils to your students. Invite them to summarize some of the most important words or phrases from their personal **Identity That Sticks** handout in the top rectangle. Give students several minutes to read the instructions and decide whether making certain choices fits or fights their desired identities, as well as the degree to which they do so. (NOTE: Let students know that just because it's listed on the handout doesn't mean it's something that "fights" against their identities. You want students to think about each item and answer honestly, which means you might want to let them know that they don't need to share their answers out loud or show their handouts to others if they don't want to.)

Real Reflections from Real Students

You can do it. You can be different. You can be a Christian on your campus and maintain your integrity and maintain your standards.

Ask: **What sorts of things on the list fit your identity?**

Ask: **What sorts of things on the list fight against your identity?**

Ask: **Now that we've talked, is there anything you'd like to change on your** Identity That Sticks **handout? Perhaps you'd like to add, edit, or delete something.** Give students a few minutes to edit their self-descriptions on their **Identity That Sticks** handouts.

HOW

Reread #4 on the **Party Trends in College** handout, *"Once students start to party, they feel 'locked in' to partying."* Ask: **Why do you think that is?**

If students haven't touched on the idea that believers who start partying perceive other Christians judging them, ask: **How do you suppose Christians' responses might contribute to other Christian college students feeling "locked in" to partying?**

Ask: **What would Jesus say about that?**

Continue: **Chances are good that today you've realized that some things you've already done—or maybe are actively involved in right now—fight against your identity in Christ more than they fit it. If you haven't heard it yet, the point of this discussion is NOT to make you feel guilty or to condemn you for those things.**

At the same time, it's appropriate for us to create space together to confess sin to God in a spirit of repentance. *Repentance* **means "turning"— turning away from sin and toward God.**

Read 1 John 1:9 to your students a few times and make sure they can see its powerful words (either on individual sheets of paper you distribute or on poster paper or a whiteboard) for the remainder of this session. Explain that you've created two different kneeling stations with pillows. Point to one station and explain it's a space for confessing choices we've made that fight against our identities. Point to the second station and explain it's a space for confessing ways we've judged others, especially other believers. Ask students to silently spend a few minutes at one, or both, of the confession stations. Consider playing mellow worship music to help set the tone.

When you're finished, gather your students together and read 1 John 1:9 one more time. Close in prayer, thanking God for his faithfulness to forgive our sins, whether they relate to partying or something else.

NOTE: If you're still meeting at the college campus, you might instead do this part outside, designating the two spots by improvising with what's available.

More Worship and Prayer

If you have time to incorporate a more active worship ritual, consider the following idea. Ahead of time you'll want to set up a large bowl (or several bowls) of water. Or if there happens to be a fountain, pond, or some other body of water near where you meet (if you're meeting on a college campus, check out the campus ahead of time for some kind of central fountain), consider doing this exercise outside instead. You'll also need a loaf of bread or a piece of pita bread—enough for each person to get a small piece.

Begin by explaining: **There's a Jewish ritual that happens once a year near the Day of Atonement. It's called** *Tashlich (pronounced TOSH-lich)*, **which means "casting off." The idea is to symbolically cast off our sins by tossing pieces of bread or food into water. As Jewish worshipers do this, they imagine the flowing water carrying the bread away as a reminder that God carries our sins away by his grace, leaving us free from carrying those burdens.**

Today we're going to do something similar as a way to symbolize our repentance, or turning away from sin and toward God. We're going to each take a piece of bread as a symbol of our sins, then we'll read a passage of Scripture together, and then we'll throw our bread into the water.

Give each student a chunk of bread and invite them all to close their eyes and consider the following: **As you hold your bread, think of it representing sin you grieve; maybe something you have held on to, maybe something you've never confessed or have never released to God. What comes to mind might have to do with the things we've talked about today that fight against your identity in Christ, or it might be something different.**

Next read out loud to students Micah 7:18-19. Read it two times, then after the second time invite students to toss their pieces of bread into the bowl and ask God to wash their sin away "into the depths of the sea." If you're able to sing or listen to a song of confession or about God's grace together, invite your students to take their time and release their pieces of bread into the bowl at some point during the song. If you're able to meet outside around a body of water, invite students to spread out as they approach the water to toss their bread in.

Close by saying: **As you've felt the freedom of releasing your sin to God, now feel the embrace of God. Know that your sins are forgiven and cast away like water going downstream. Because of Christ, you are reconciled to God. Because of Christ, we are reconciled to one another. We are new creations!** (2 Corinthians 5:17).

PARTY TRENDS IN COLLEGE

1. Having a moral "to do" (or perhaps more accurately, a "not to do") list doesn't cut it.

2. Who you hang out with in college makes a huge difference.

3. Many college freshmen party primarily because they want to make friends.

4. Once students start to party, they feel "locked in" to partying.

5. It's not "if" you'll have the opportunity to party and have sex and drink alcohol, but "when."

FIT OR FIGHT?

In the rectangle below, write down the major phrases or words from your **Identity That Sticks** handout.

Next read the following choices and decide if that action fits or fights with who you want to be as described in the rectangle. Then place an X on the spot that marks the degree it fits or fights. On a scale of 1-5, 1 is a minor fit or fight, and 5 is a major fit or fight.

	Major Fit			Minor Fit		Minor Fight			Major Fight	
	5	4	3	2	1	1	2	3	4	5
Telling someone I'm going to a party										
Inviting others to a party										
Walking past a party										
Walking into a party										
Holding an alcoholic drink in your hand										
Drinking some alcohol										
Drinking a lot of alcohol										
Being offered some drugs										
Doing a few drugs										
Doing a lot of drugs										

	Major Fit			Minor Fit		Minor Fight			Major Fight	
	5	4	3	2	1	1	2	3	4	5
Looking at a little pornography										
Looking at a lot of pornography										
Experimenting with homosexuality										
Flirting with a stranger										
Flirting with someone I know										
Kissing someone a little bit										
Kissing someone a lot										
Masturbating with someone										
Having oral sex										
Having sexual intercourse										

8

how can i find a new church?

The Big Idea:

Finding a church or fellowship group after graduation is important to Sticky Faith.

You'll Need:

Optional: Photos (or even a slide show or video) that will trigger students' memories of what you've shared together. Odds are good you'll be doing this at some point before they graduate so you might as well get a jump on it now.

Pizza

Plates and napkins

Bibles

Copies of the **Questions about a Church or College Group** handout on page 98

Ideally, a handful of computers with Internet access

To research churches or fellowship groups near your students' future colleges, homes, or jobs. Some helpful Web links are listed in the **How** section; you might also want to look for churches or fellowship groups through your denominational network.

Ahead of time create a handout with the Web links in the **How** section, as well as any other denominational online information that you locate, and make copies for your students.

Invite whoever leads your college ministry to come for this meeting, at least for the final portion, as well as your senior pastor or some other adult in leadership (particularly if you don't have a college ministry) who can participate in the last part of the session, too.

Copies of students' previously completed **Identity That Sticks** handouts from session two

More Worship and Prayer Option: Pencils and paper

NOW

Greet your students and get the conversation rolling by asking, **What will you miss about our youth group after you graduate?** If you'd like, distribute photos or play your slide show/video to help students reflect on the memories you've shared.

Whether or not you show photos or slides, share a few stories of some of your fondest memories about these seniors. Try to have at least one of those stories demonstrate how students have grown spiritually as you've journeyed together.

Continue: **Let's be honest with each other: Once you graduate, whether or not you stay connected with our church or get connected to a new one or drift from church altogether will be up to you. Nearly half of seniors who graduate from youth groups like ours end up drifting from the church.[1] That's one out of two. Why do you think that is?**

At some point as students are answering that question, get out your pizza. But before you hand out slices to students, explain: **Imagine this pizza is piping hot—way too hot to eat. In fact, it's so hot that if you ate it, it would burn** your mouth. Begin putting individual slices on plates as you continue: **Short of putting the pizza in the refrigerator, I might try to cool it off by doing what I'm doing now and take individual pieces and put them on plates so they can cool separately. Each piece of pizza will cool more quickly if it's on its own.**

Hand out the pizza to students to eat as you ask: **How is that similar to what might happen to you if you drift from the church and Christian community after you graduate?**

NEW

At this point distribute Bibles and invite students to turn to Philippians 2:12-13. As they are doing so, explain: **My goal is not to make you feel so guilty that you'll get connected with a church or faith community after you graduate. Nor is it to scare you into doing so. Instead my goal is to show you how connecting with a faith community will help you by allowing you to be the person you want to be after you graduate.**

Ask for a volunteer to read Philippians 2:12-13. Walk students through the passage by making the following points and asking the following questions: **Note that this passage starts with the word** *therefore.* **Given that, we need to look backward in the text to see what is causing Paul's "therefore." What does Paul describe in Philippians 2:5-11, and what's the connection to verses 12-13?**

    The phrase "work out your salvation" has been very confusing to folks throughout history. Some believe it means to "work *for* **your salvation."** (Feel free to refer back to what you discussed in session one on the gospel as you help students better understand that salvation by our work is impossible; it's Jesus' work on the

Real Reflections from Real Students

One youth group graduate who ended up being the president of her college campus fellowship reported, "I think one of the main reasons I got so involved in ministry was the first week I was on campus I was looking for one because my youth pastor encouraged me that I needed to find community as soon as possible. Don't put it on the back burner and don't skip church that first week, because it just makes it easier to skip it the second week and then the eighth week."

91

cross that makes our salvation possible.) **Even if we realize that Paul doesn't mean we should work "for" our salvation, it still can be tough to tell what Paul means by working "out" your salvation. What do you think Paul is after?**

This isn't an easy concept to understand, but the essence of Paul's teaching is that once we choose to follow Jesus, we are saved. And yet, every day we continue to figure out and live out that new life in Christ.

NOTE: One comparison that might be helpful is to explain that it's like being accepted to a college. You're accepted the day the school writes you the acceptance letter. But then for the next four years (or in some cases, five or six or even seven years . . .), you "work out" (or experience) what it means to be a college student.

Continue: **I want you to remember a few things when it comes to working out your salvation. First, these few verses are written to an entire group of Jesus followers. Second, I want you to think about the way our pizza slices cooled down when they were separated from each other. Given that, what role do you think other believers could play in you continuing to work out your salvation after you graduate?**

The big theme for today is that we don't have to live out our salvation alone. God wants us to live in community with other followers of Jesus. And even as you're graduating, the good news for all of us is that the more we in this youth ministry continue to stay in touch, the more likely it is that you'll have Sticky Faith.[2]

As your youth leader, I want to keep in touch with you. If you have a sense of how you'd like to keep in touch with your seniors (i.e., via email, social networking, phone calls, a dinner reunion at winter break), now would be a good time to share that. **And hopefully you know you can contact me any time.**

HOW

Continue: **Having said that, the reality is that I can't go to your college or job or next city with you. I really want you to connect with other adults in** a church or college group who can be part of the next chapter God has for you. In fact, the Sticky Faith research shows that connecting with older adults is part of what helps you develop Sticky Faith.

■ Continue: **The people who can help you live out your salvation can be found in a local church or college ministry. Yet one of the top three difficulties seniors face when they graduate is finding a church or college group.**[3]

■ Continue: **To help each of you find a church, we're going to talk about the types of questions we should ask ourselves, and others, as we try to find a group that fits how God is helping us live out our salvation.**

Distribute pencils and copies of the **Questions about a Church or College Group** handout and review it with your students. Be sure to highlight what's written at the top of the handout: There are no "right" answers. Some of your students will be drawn to a large group; others will prefer a smaller group. For some worship is a priority; for others, serving the poor gets top billing. The point is not to selfishly ask, "What can this church/group do for me?" but "How can God help me 'work out my salvation' through this church/group?"

NOTE: At the bottom of the handout is a space for "other" questions. Ask: **What else would you want to know about a campus group or church?**

■ Ask: **It seems as though asking these questions could make us almost too picky, or feel more like customers trying to "purchase" something as opposed to followers of Christ trying to find a group to help them live out their salvation. How can you ask these questions but keep an open, humble attitude?**

■ Explain: **Youth group graduates like you often wish that their youth leader had done**

Real Reflections from Real Students

I got involved in a college group, and then I realized it was wrong for me and at that point I was a bit disillusioned about the whole idea. I didn't really feel like going out and looking for another one and having the same negative experience. So before you get involved in the college group, before you get emotionally invested, make sure it's right for you and find people who're going to help you grow as a Christian. Once you find that group, get involved and stick with it.

Real Reflections from Real Students

While youth group seniors are in high school, they should try to research churches in the area of their college . . . because it's really hard to do it on your own.

a better job helping them find a church or college group.[4] I don't want you to wish later on that I had done more to help you, so we're going to look for churches and college groups together today.

At this point, show students the computers with online access and explain: **Using these computers, as well as your own phones, let's explore which churches and college groups are close to where you'll be living or working after graduation.** Distribute the handouts you've prepared with the links, as well as any other links you've added. (NOTE: The reason we haven't made these links into a handout is that while the Web addresses are accurate as of the date of the printing of this book, they may change by the time you're using this session. So please double-check these links and do a bit of research yourself before distributing them to your students. Feel free to add links connected with your own church, ministry, or denominational affiliation.)

General Database Of College Ministries

www.liveabove.com

Fellowship Groups That Tend To Meet On College Campuses

Campus Crusade for Christ (now known as "Cru"):
   www.ccci.org
InterVarsity Christian Fellowship: www.intervarsity.org/chapters
The Navigators: http.navigators.org/us/ministries/college/
   campus-locator
Young Life College: www.younglife.org/Locator/Default.htm?Search
   By=Ministry&SearchFor=College

NOTE: If your denomination sponsors a particular campus ministry (e.g.,

Christian Reformed Campus Ministry or Wesley Foundation), please research it ahead of time and add that to this list as well.

■ After you distribute the handouts, explain: **My hope is that each of you finds one, if not a handful, of ministries located near where you're going to live or attend college. On this handout, jot down any contact information or meeting schedules posted online.**

If none of the links relate to where you'll be after graduation, then simply Google your city, as well as the word *church*, **to see what pops up. Feel free to also include our denomination in that online search. Click through the search results to check out the churches' individual Web sites. Jot down on this handout the name, location, and meeting schedule of any churches that seem interesting to you.**

Give each student a chance to share one ministry or church that he or she thought appealing. If a student hasn't found something, then commit to that student that you'll work with him or her in the next week to find a church or ministry near where he or she will be living or working—and then make sure to follow through.

Have More Time?

At this point, introduce the leader of your church's college ministry and give your students a chance to introduce themselves to him or her. Point out that even if your students will be living elsewhere for the school year, they're likely to come home for breaks and summer vacation, so it's a good idea for them to find out more about your church's college ministry. Give your church's college leader time to explain the mission and programs of your church's college ministry and field questions.

If there's no college ministry and/or no college leader at your church, invite your senior pastor or another key adult leader to come and share their enthusiasm for involving youth group graduates even more fully into the life of your church.

Hopefully you've also worked out some sort of plan for the summer to help graduates transition from the youth ministry to church events and/or your church's college ministry. Now would be a good time to explain that plan to your students.

If you have time, distribute copies of the *Identity That Sticks* handout that students completed in session two. Give students a few minutes to edit and expand their descriptions of themselves at the bottom of the handout in regard to how they want to get connected to a church or parachurch ministry in college. Invite a few volunteers to share any changes or additions they've made to their visions of themselves a year from now.

Close by asking your college ministry leader or pastor to pray for your students' Sticky Faith, that God will help them stay connected not only to God, but also to a vital Christian community that helps them live out their salvation.

More Worship and Prayer

If you have time to incorporate more space for reflection, consider inviting students to connect their need for a church with the importance of intergenerational relationships. Introduce this exercise by saying: **Remember back in the second session when we talked about our identities and looked at a list of biblical names God has given us? The bigger truth about those names is that all of them are given not just to individuals but to the WHOLE people of God, the whole church. So when Scripture says we are beloved or chosen or holy, it applies to us individually but is also spoken to God-followers collectively, just like the Philippians passage we read earlier.**

As we noted, you're more likely to have Sticky Faith when you have relationships not just with people your own age but with adults who are older and even kids who are younger. So let's get more specific . . .

At this point hand out pieces of paper and pens to students. Instruct them to divide the paper into four quadrants by drawing a line down the middle horizontally and another down the middle vertically. Then say: **Over the next few minutes I'd like you to brainstorm lists of people of different ages in the church who are part of your web of Sticky Faith relationships. Let's** go through the quadrants and label them, then I'll give you time to make lists. Walk students through the following categories, then give them time to write down names on each list:

1. Older "senior" adults—like your grandparents' ages—who you are connected with in the church
2. Adults around your parents' ages or younger, probably including most of your youth leaders
3. Peers around your own age
4. Younger kids—middle school, elementary age, or younger who you are connected with in some way

After students have finished listing names, continue: **Now look at your lists. Where are there more names? Where is there more blank space?**

Let's take some time to pray silently through your lists. Pray for the people who are already on your lists, that they would continue to be part of your faith family as you grow into the next phase of being part of the church. Then pray that God would bring new people into your life to fill out the short lists, and if you're going away to college, that God would add to your lists from each age group to continue to help you work out your salvation.

QUESTIONS ABOUT A CHURCH OR COLLEGE GROUP

As you're visiting different churches or college groups, keep in mind the following questions. (You can probably think of additional questions that are important to you, and you can add those at the bottom of this list.)

There are no "right" answers to these questions. You might love large gatherings, or you might be drawn to smaller times of worship. You might want to meet on Sunday mornings, or you might want to attend Wednesday night gatherings. The key is to prayerfully and thoughtfully identify a church or college group that matches who you are and that can help you develop Sticky Faith.

What is the mission or vision of this group?

Where does this group meet? How am I going to get there?

When does this group meet? How does that fit my schedule?

How many people are involved?

Of those who are involved, how many are my gender and/or year in school and/or ethnicity? How much similarity or difference is important?

Who leads this group? How do I connect with the leader(s)?

What's the teaching like?

How about the worship?

Are there small groups or Bible studies that are part of this group?

What does this group do to reach out to people who don't know Jesus yet?

What does this group do to help those who are poor or marginalized?

How can I use my gifts and talents as part of this group?

How much does this group spend time together outside of gatherings?

Other questions that are important to you?

9

how can i manage my life after high school?

The Big Idea:

Setting schedule and budget priorities now will pay off later.

You'll Need:

Three jars, three bowls, rocks, and sand. Ahead of time, fill each jar with rocks, and then add as much sand as you can until each jar is completely full. Dump the contents of each jar into its own bowl and then refill each jar with only the sand that it contained. Leave the rocks in the bowls and make sure you keep track of which bowl (with rocks) goes with which jar.

Paper

Pens or pencils

Whiteboard or poster paper

Markers

Bibles

Copies of the **My Schedule** and the **My Monthly Budget** handouts on pages 105–106 and 107–108
Copies of students' previously completed **Identity That Sticks**
handouts from session two

NOW

Greet your students and find out how their days are going. Share about your day. Do an actual rundown of all you've done so far today (if you're meeting in the morning, describe what you did yesterday).

Distribute pencils and blank paper and ask: **What about you? How have you spent the last 24 hours? Write down your schedule for the last 24 hours, the best you can remember.**

When students are finished, see if any want to share about how they spent their last day. Ask: **If I hadn't met you yet, and all I knew about you was how you spent your last 24 hours, what would I conclude was important to you?**

Ask: **High school students are in class about 35 hours a week. If you plan to attend college, that number will change to more like 15 hours a week. Graduating seniors often feel especially unprepared to handle the new choices they have about their time.**[1] As one student said, "In high school, *everything* was scheduled. In college, I was finished with classes by noon and had all day to do whatever I wanted." **You'll have a lot more time, and probably a lot less parental input on how you spend it. Finding the right balance can be difficult; so difficult, in fact, that it causes some students to drop out.**[2]

Continue: **Graduating seniors also have trouble navigating their new choices in another area: their money.**[3] **Let's start by thinking about how you're handling your money right now.** Invite students to flip over their sheets of paper and conduct a financial inventory of their bedrooms at home, listing items in their rooms and the approximate cost of each. Include clothes, furniture, books, and electronics. Have them total up the "value" of their room.

▪ Ask the same question you asked about time earlier: **If I hadn't met you yet, and all I knew about you was what was in your room, what would I think is important to you?**

▪ Ask: **How will your financial situation be different after you graduate?** Make sure you remind students that they're likely to be offered more financial options, such as checking accounts and credit cards, that can be enticing but can lead to great debt.

▪ Transition: **The point of tracking our schedules and inventorying our rooms is not to make us feel guilty about how much clothing we have or how much time we spent playing video games yesterday; it's to make us aware of and get us thinking about ways we can manage our money and time so that God is honored and pleased.**

NEW

▪ Divide your students into groups and give each group a jar with sand as well as their corresponding bowl filled with rocks.[4] Explain: **The goal is to fit all the rocks in the jar. Go.**

Odds are good that students will futilely attempt to stuff their rocks into their jars without fully emptying their jars of sand. Only when the sand is first emptied so that the rocks are placed inside first will all of the rocks and sand fit in the jar.

▪ When each group has realized this and filled their jars with the rocks first and then the sand, ask: **What can we learn from the rocks and the sand?**

Real Reflections from Real Students

Compared to high school, I now know more about myself and less about what I believe than I used to. I hope this will resolve at some point in my life. I want it to, but at this point it's on hold because I don't have the time or the tools. It's hard to find time to think about religion or God, and college feels more like living from one day to the next and losing focus on big-picture things.

Ask: **How does what happened with the rocks and the sand relate to the way we manage our money and our time?**

Ask: **What are some of the "rocks" that are important to God in terms of what we spend our time on? In other words, how do you suppose God wants us to spend our time?** List students' answers on the whiteboard or poster paper.

Distribute Bibles and explain: **Let's see how the time "rocks" you came up with match what we know from Scripture.** Ask for volunteers to read the following Scripture passages. (NOTE: Feel free to delete some of these or add other passages that you believe are "rock"-ish; this is by no means an exhaustive list):

> Psalm 31:5
> Esther 4:14
> Mark 1:35
> Luke 10:38-42

Ask: **What do you notice about the time "rocks" we identified in light of what we read in Scripture? Based on what we read from Scripture and what we know about Kingdom living, what "big rock" practices or attitudes would you add to this list related to how we use our time?**

Scripture Sidebar

In Luke 10:38-42, we read that Mary sat at Jesus' feet. Perhaps part of why this description of Mary seems unattainable in our culture today is because our schedules and personalities often don't lend themselves to physically sitting and connecting with Jesus for hours on end. While focused and regular connections with Jesus are important to our spiritual journeys, in the first century, "sitting at someone's feet" also meant following them every day—as disciples would follow their rabbis. So while Mary's model invites us to literally sit and experience Jesus, Luke 10:38-42 also prods us to ask: How can we experience Jesus in everything we do?

Ask: **What sorts of things keep us from attending to the "big rocks" in life?**

Similarly, ask: **What are some of the "rocks" that are important to God in terms of how we spend our money? In other words, how do you suppose God wants us to use our money?** List students' answers on the whiteboard or poster paper.

Distribute Bibles and explain: **Let's see how the money "rocks" you came up with match what we know from Scripture.** Ask for volunteers to read the following Scripture passages. (NOTE: Again, feel free to delete some of these or add other passages that you believe are "rock"-ish; this is by no means an exhaustive list):

> *Real Reflections from Real Students*
>
> There's gonna be a definite shift in terms of your freedom to decide how you want to live each day and prioritize what's most important to you. The whole "seek first his Kingdom and his righteousness, and all these things will be added to you as well" is true as all get-out.

Psalm 24:1-2
Matthew 6:19-21
1 Corinthians 16:2
2 Corinthians 9:6-8
Philippians 4:11-13

Ask: **What do you notice about the money "rocks" we identified in light of what we read in Scripture? Based on what we read from Scripture and what we know about Kingdom living, what "big rock" practices or attitudes would you add to our list related to how we steward our money?**

Ask: **What sorts of things keep us from putting our money toward the "big rocks"?**

HOW

Explain: **Now I'd like us to get personal and think about how we'd like to include these "rocks" in our budgets and schedules after we graduate. Even if you'll ultimately keep track of your schedule and your budget on your phone or computer, sometimes it's helpful to map it out on paper first.**

Distribute copies of **My Schedule** and ask students to follow the directions and each fill out the schedule they'd like to keep after they graduate. If you have time, when students are finished, ask questions like: **What made this exercise challenging? What was especially hard to fit in? How do you feel about the schedule you've designed?**

Distribute copies of **My Monthly Budget** and ask students to follow the directions and each design a potential budget. If you have time, after students have completed their potential budgets, ask: **What made this exercise difficult? What are you concerned about in your budget? What are you looking forward to in your budget?**

If you have time, distribute copies of the *Identity That Sticks* handout that students completed in session two. Give students a few minutes to edit and expand their descriptions of themselves at the bottom of the handout in regard to how they want their faith to influence their schedules and finances. Invite a few volunteers to share any changes or additions they've made to their visions of themselves a year from now.

When you're finished, invite each student to pull out a rock from a nearby jar. Have them each hold a rock in their hand as you close in prayer, asking God to help each of you keep God's "rocks" at the center of your budget and schedule.

MY SCHEDULE

List the "rocks" that you believe God would like you to include in your schedule:

List the "sand" that you'd also like to include:

In the schedule (next page), first map out your "rocks" and then add your "sand." A few tips to help you:

Typically a college student is in class 12-15 hours/week.

You should also block off time for studying outside of class.

Make sure you also factor your job or any ongoing ministry or church commitments.

	Sunday	Monday	Tuesday	Wednesday	Thursday	Friday	Saturday
6 am							
7 am							
8 am							
9 am							
10 am							
11 am							
noon							
1 pm							
2 pm							
3 pm							
4 pm							
5 pm							
6 pm							
7 pm							
8 pm							
9 pm							
10 pm							
11 pm							
midnight							
1 am							

MY MONTHLY BUDGET

List the "rocks" you believe God wants you to include
in your budget:

List the "sand" you'd also like to add:

Complete the monthly budget (next page), making your most educated guesses. You
can certainly revisit this budget in the future.

Total monthly income _____

Minus taxes (approximately 20 percent of income) _____

Minus tithe (approximately 10 percent of income) _____

Available income: _____

Expenses _____

Housing _____

Food _____

Auto (payment, insurance, registration, and gas) _____

Savings and/or debt payoff _____

Clothing _____

Utilities _____

Entertainment _____

Other/Miscellaneous _____

Total expenses _____

NOTE: Total expenses must be less than or equal to total income.

10

how can i experience god on a regular basis?

The Big Idea:

Consistent personal faith practices or "disciplines" lay the groundwork for faith that sticks beyond the structured discipleship of your high school youth ministry.

You'll Need:

To find on DVD or online the film clip from *Akeelah and the Bee* called "Small Words" (length: 3:29). At the time of publication, it can be found on YouTube at http://www.youtube.com/watch?v=ZQ2UdNY0UAw.

Copies of the handout, **Spiritual Disciplines: Sticky Pathways of Grace** handout on pages 116–118 for each student

Pens/pencils

Copies of the **Prayer of Examen** handout on pages 119–120 for each student

NOW

Welcome students, check in with one another, and then introduce the session: **We're going to watch a clip from the film** *Akeelah and the Bee* **about an 11-year-old girl who discovers a capacity she has for spelling that launches her from her inner-city neighborhood into training for the National Spelling Bee. In this clip, we see Akeelah working with her new coach, played by Laurence Fishburne. They clearly disagree about the best method to help Akeelah win the bee.**

Play the clip, then ask the following questions to start discussion.

What was driving Akeelah's argument with Dr. Larabee?

What did she learn about training for the bee that surprised her?

Akeelah had a clear driving motivation—to win the National Spelling Bee. But she didn't understand how to go about training in a way that would help her accomplish her goal. Even though we're not trying to win a spelling bee right now, the same principle holds true for us: learning big things or growing in big ways usually requires lots of little steps, or in this case, little words.

Ask: **What do you think of when you hear the terms** *spiritual disciplines* **or** *faith practices*? **Are those familiar or unfamiliar terms?**

Ask: **What are some examples of spiritual disciplines or practices you know of?** Students might think of prayer, worship, Bible study, or serving the poor. If they can't think of anything, they may not quite get the question, so you may want to supply one or two examples to get them started. Let them know that they'll get to look at a list later that might include some examples they haven't heard or haven't thought of as disciplines.

Ask: **How is practicing spiritual disciplines like learning the "small words"?**

Say: **In the same way that learning small words helps us learn the roots on which more complex language is built, prayer and other disciplines give us basic spiritual grounding on which to build a more complex and truly Sticky Faith.**

110

Then say: **Research shows that faith practices *are*, in fact, important to Sticky Faith. Worshiping with others is linked to faith maturity, both in high school and across the transition to college. Being part of a church or campus ministry in college— where you practice faith with others—is also connected with Sticky Faith.**[1]

Yet often students aren't sure how to nurture their own spiritual growth in college. They don't pray or read their Bibles much. They don't have ideas for other faith practices that might make a difference in their day-to-day lives.

> ### *Real Reflections from Real Students*
>
> To youth pastors: Don't be afraid to ask your kids difficult questions now and push them to ask difficult questions; challenge them with big ideas and definitely challenge them to build disciplined habits that will shape them in the future and expect a lot from them, because they can do a lot.

NEW

Continue: **There are a number of practices Christians have used through the centuries to connect with God, but many spiritual leaders would suggest that at the core of all of the disciplines is the practice of prayer. So let's focus for a few minutes just on prayer.**

Ask: **Think for a few moments about your own prayer tendencies. What makes you want to pray, and when do you usually pray?**

Continue: **We've made prayer into something that's primarily about *intercession*—in other words, trying to get God to do something or sometimes to give us something. This isn't all bad, but the foundation of a life of prayer isn't really about asking God for anything; *it's about simply being with God.* This is what ancient believers called "holy leisure"—a condition of the soul where we're fully alive and aware of wonder in the world and open to God's presence.**[2]

Leisure is from a Latin root (a small word) meaning "to be given freedom," so we can think about prayer as holy space where we're set free to become aware of God's love and power in our lives.

Ask: **What do you think of that approach to prayer?**

At this point you might want to point out that the challenge with prayer—or any discipline—is avoiding the predictable pattern of setting up legalistic rituals that cause us to depend more on our behaviors for favor with God than on God's grace through Christ's sacrifice on our behalf.

Remind students that, as we explored in the What's the Real Gospel? session, the Christian faith is not about knowing and doing right things to get points with God; rather it's about experiencing God's incredible grace. Prayer can be one of the most important channels through which we experience God's grace.

This is also an appropriate time to share a personal story about your own experiences with prayer and other spiritual disciplines. If you've prayed more out of a sense of obligation or because someone "guilted" you into having a "daily quiet time," what has helped you counter that kind of attitude? On the flip side, what regular practices (quiet time or otherwise) have helped you experience God's grace and presence?

Continue: **"Just being with Jesus" sounds simple, but often we make it harder than that. Maybe it's because we feel like prayer should always be "productive" in some way and lead to results we can see or feel. In contrast, listen to the way** *The Message* **version of the Bible describes Jesus' words in Matthew 11:29-30:**

"Walk with me and work with me—watch how I do it. *Learn the unforced rhythms of grace.* I won't lay anything heavy or ill-fitting on you. Keep company with me and you'll learn to live freely and lightly" (emphasis added).

Ask: **What do you think Jesus means by "unforced rhythms of grace"? Is this the way you normally think about discipleship or spiritual disciplines?**

HOW

Ask: **So if spiritual disciplines are pathways to grace, and grace is what transforms**

Real Reflections from Real Students

I think a lot of times in high school people go to church because their parents drag them along. When you get to college it's your own faith, it's time to choose, you choose to go to church and read the Bible on your own, just like studying for classes. You should study the Bible, only realize that the Bible is so much more important than any other class that you are studying for.

College students in Fuller's College Transition Project research have reported the following as obstacles to engaging in faith practices:

Time: Making space for God in the midst of balancing other priorities and managing your own schedule is tough.

Relationships: Suddenly you don't know other Christians and have to decide if you're going to show up by yourself at a campus group or church. You also may not have accountability relationships with people who remind you to stay connected in your faith.

Faith: God may begin to seem distant, uninvolved, or even irrelevant to college life.

us to be like Christ, what keeps us from practicing prayer and other disciplines?

This isn't a simple answer, but it's good to get students thinking about the factors. Part of our lack of discipline is because we don't make time for it (perhaps because down deep we don't think it's that important), but part of it is also because we don't know how to pray, or we don't believe we're doing it the right way.

Ask: **What do you suppose are some of the obstacles to faith practices in college? What do you suppose "gets in the way"?**

Continue: **I know that in my own life, part of why I don't engage in spiritual disciplines as much as I'd like to is that I forget that there are a lot of different ways to stay connected to God.** Distribute the **Spiritual Disciplines: Sticky Pathways of Grace** handout and read aloud the instructions at the top. Give students individual reflection time, then gather them back together (or in smaller groups if you have a large group) to discuss the reflection questions at the end before moving into the prayer activity.

More Worship and Prayer

Unlike some of the sessions where this part is optional, *we highly encourage you to close your session with this prayer exercise* as a way to equip students with a skill they can use themselves in their own prayer times.

113

Many students may have little or no experience beyond basic prayers of thanksgiving, petition, and intercession ("God, thanks for my day. Please help me not fail my math test, and help Grandma feel better"). Instead, this guide is based on what's known as the Ignatian *Prayer of Examen*, or *Prayer of Review*. The ancient practice is simply a way to review our day before God and recognize our "highs and lows," offering them to God. If this approach to prayer is new to you, you may want to access some of the following resources ahead of time:

Dennis Linn, Sheila Linn, and Matthew Linn, *Sleeping with Bread: Holding What Gives You Life* (New York: Paulist, 1995).
http://www.pray-as-you-go.org/
http://norprov.org/spirituality/ignatianprayer.htm
Really any online search for "prayer of examen" is going to give you ideas— it's widely practiced in and outside of the Jesuit tradition.

Often this prayer is led out loud, but we've created a handout called **Prayer of Examen** for you to distribute to students at this time. You may either lead it out loud and give students the handout as a reference, or let them guide themselves through the prayer silently. The advantage of leading out loud is that students get a better feel for the slow pacing through the various steps as you model it, but please do whatever seems best for your context. Set up this prayer time by saying something like:

We're going to spend some extended time in prayer to close out this session, but this prayer might be a little different from what you're used to. In this prayer we are going to invite God to help us reflect on our day and listen for what God has been doing in and around us. Don't worry if you're not sure whether you're doing the prayer "right" or not—the important thing is just to make space to slow down and be present with God.

Invite students to take a handout, spread out from one another, and get comfortable as they begin the prayer exercise. Let them know at the start how much time you'll give them (we suggest about 10 minutes if this kind of prayer is new to students). Make sure you and any other adults present also practice the prayer during this time, whether you're leading it out loud or silently.

Be sure to give students a two-minute warning to wrap up their prayer before bringing the group back together, then take time to debrief with the following questions:

What was this like for you?

How was God present? What did you notice about God through this process?

What, if anything, did God reveal to you during the prayer? Invite students to share anything that may have come out of their experiences, but don't push if that sharing isn't coming freely.

What could it be like to use this prayer each day, or each week? Do you suppose this way of praying could be a helpful practice for you in college? Why or why not?

Close by reminding students that the desire to be with God and seek after God is more pleasing to God than any prayer method or spiritual practice in itself, and encourage them to explore new practices in the coming week. Then send them out with this quote from Mother Teresa (included on the bottom of their **Prayer of Examen** handout):

> We need to find God, and he cannot be found in noise and restlessness. God is the friend of silence . . . the more we receive in silent prayer, the more we can give in our active life.[3]

SPIRITUAL DISCIPLINES: STICKY PATHWAYS OF GRACE

Walk with me and work with me—watch how I do it. Learn the unforced rhythms of grace. I won't lay anything heavy or ill-fitting on you. Keep company with me and you'll learn to live freely and lightly.

Matthew 11:29-30, The Message

There are all kinds of ways people have sought to be with God and pursue the presence of God through Christian history. The following list of "classic" spiritual disciplines (or practices) is only a sample of the pathways toward experiencing God's grace.[*] Read through this list and:

<u>Underline</u> any you've already practiced or participated in.

(Circle) one or two you've never experienced but might want to try.

Meditation: The discipline of slowing down and cutting out all the noise so you can focus your heart and mind on Jesus Christ. It might include imagining yourself with Jesus or just thinking about God's love.

Prayer: The practice of listening to and talking with God, not just when you fold your hands and close your eyes, but any and every time you communicate or simply commune with God.

Study: The discipline of searching for the truth of God through the Scriptures, creation, church tradition, and the wisdom of saints who've gone before you.

Fasting: The discipline of abstaining from something and being filled instead by the presence of God. It could include abstaining from food, your iPod, Facebook, or anything else you use for fulfillment.

Journaling: The practice of writing down your thoughts and prayers toward God, including meditations on Scripture and life experiences.

---

[*] This list of disciplines and their descriptions are adapted from Richard Foster's *Celebration of Discipline* (San Francisco: HarperCollins, 1978).

Simplicity: The discipline of living without being enslaved to your "stuff" (i.e., cars, clothes, phone, bling . . .). Simplicity is about being free from the control of materialism so you can freely give to and receive from others.

Solitude: The practice of being alone and facing your loneliness as you encounter God. Solitude allows you to face yourself and come face-to-face with God without the comfort or distraction of others.

Submission: The discipline of denying yourself, often to give to another, not out of duty but in love and freedom. It can include giving up your power, possessions, comfort, opinions, and even your life for the sake of others.

Service/Seeking Justice: The act of humbling yourself and serving the needs of others. Jesus modeled this discipline in washing his disciples' feet. Sometimes this means seeking to change systems and injustices that oppress people and keep them from becoming whole.

Confession: The discipline of confessing your sins and temptations to a trusted believer. In confession, you're able to forgive and bear with another as you experience God's grace and forgiveness. Sometimes we call this "accountability" when we confess to others and ask them to hold us accountable for our sins as well as our disciplines.

Worship: The practice of acknowledging God's presence and responding to God's grace, beauty, and love. Worship can be expressed in silence, in song, in creating art or playing in God's creation.

Guidance/Discernment: The act of seeking the wisdom of others for direction in your life and spiritual journey. It involves seeking the guidance of the Holy Spirit through the voice of a faithful community (trusted friends and family who love and follow God; pastors or mentors; etc.).

Celebration: The practice of partying! Remember, the gospel literally means "good news." You have every reason to celebrate God's goodness, enjoy God's creation, and embrace the people God has put in your life.

REFLECTION

1.Look back at the spiritual discipline(s) you **underlined** (the ones you've done before). What joys or struggles have they brought to your spiritual life? What could you try in the coming months to experience God's presence through practicing one of these disciplines in a fresh and new way as you prepare for college? What about once you get to college?

2. Look at the spiritual discipline(s) you (circled) (those you've never done but might want to try). How could you explore one of these disciplines in the coming months as you prepare for college? What would it take to keep practicing this discipline in college? Who could you ask to practice this new spiritual discipline with you?

*** Remember, the desire to be with God and seek after God is more pleasing to God than any prayer method or spiritual practice in itself. So if you try any discipline and "fail," simply reaffirm to God, "I want to be with you" and let that be enough.

PRAYER OF EXAMEN

This guide is based on what's known as the Ignatian *Prayer of Examen*, or *Prayer of Review*. The ancient practice is simply a way to review your day before God and recognize your "highs and lows," offering them to God. In this prayer we'll first take a few moments to quiet ourselves, and then we'll invite God to help us reflect on our day and listen for what God might want to do in and through us in the coming days. Don't worry if you're not sure what to say to God during these moments—the important part is simply being present with God, just as God is present with you. Please GO SLOWLY, only moving to the next step when you feel ready.

1. **Slow Down:** Take a moment now to stop, to become still and focused. Let your breathing help you relax as you breathe in and out. Imagine you're breathing out distractions and anxieties and breathing in the presence and peace of God.

2. **Invite:** As you begin the prayer, ask God to guide your thoughts, feelings, and reactions so you might see God's presence in your life. You can do this by simply praying, "I give this time to you," or "I want to be with you."

3. **Review:** And now slowly begin to recall the day, as if you were walking back through your life today as an observer:

   How did you feel when you woke up this morning and during the first part of the day?

   What was happening? Where did you go? What did you do? Who were you with? What sort of mood were you in?

   Continue walking through your day. How did you spend your afternoon? Where were you? Who were you with? What was happening? How did you feel?

   Now let your memory drift over your evening, also recalling events, people, and feelings.

4. **Notice Your "Highs":** For what are you most grateful today? What was most life-giving to you? Where or when did God seem most present? Give thanks to God for that gift.

5. Uncover Your "Lows": For what are you least grateful today? What was most life-draining for you? Where did you least sense God's presence? Speak with God about that, too.

6. Rest with God: Close this time by silently having a conversation with God about the day, offering both highs and lows back to God's care and asking that you might experience God's presence and grace more in the coming day.

> We need to find God, and he cannot be found in noise and restlessness. God is the friend of silence . . . the more we receive in silent prayer, the more we can give in our active life.[*]   *Mother Teresa*

---

[*] Mother Teresa, quoted in Malcolm Muggeridge, *Something Beautiful for God* (New York: Ballantine Books, 1979), 48.

notes

Introduction

1. In September 2006, the Barna Group released their observation that "the most potent data regarding disengagement is that a majority of twentysomethings—61 percent of today's young adults—had been churched at one point during their teen years but they are now spiritually disengaged." *Barna Update*, "Most Twentysomethings Put Christianity on the Shelf Following Spiritually Active Teen Years," *The Barna Group*, 2006, September 16, 2006. According to a Gallup Poll, approximately 40 percent of 18-29 year-olds who attended church when they were 16 or 17 years old are no longer attending. George H. Gallup, Jr. "The Religiosity Cycle," *The Gallup Poll*, 2002, October 19, 2006. Frank Newport, "A Look at Religious Switching in America Today," *The Gallup Poll*, 2006, October 19, 2006.

   A 2007 survey by LifeWay Research of more than 1,000 adults ages 18-30 who spent a year or more in youth group during high school suggests that more than 65 percent of young adults who attend a Protestant church for at least a year in high school will stop attending church regularly for at least a year between the ages of 18 and 22. In this study, respondents were not necessarily seniors who had graduated from youth group. In addition, the research design did not factor in parachurch or on-campus faith communities in their definition of college "church" attendance.

   Data from the National Study of Youth and Religion published in 2009 indicate an approximate 30 percent drop in frequent religious service attendance across multiple Protestant denominations. Christian Smith with Patricia Snell, *Souls in Transition: The Religious & Spiritual Lives of Emerging Adults* (New York: Oxford University Press, 2009).

   Fuller Youth Institute estimates that 40-50 percent of high school graduates will fail to stick with their faith is based on a compilation of data from these various studies.

2. Fuller Youth Institute College Transition Project. For more on the research and implications for youth ministry and parents, see stickyfaith.org and other Sticky Faith books in this series: *Sticky Faith* and *Sticky Faith: Youth Worker Edition*.

3. We wrestled with how to describe the fact that God cares about and interacts with each individual, and yet much of our faith growth is communal. *Personal* is our best attempt, but by using that term, we do not mean to imply an individualistic faith.

4. See originally Chap Clark and Kara Powell, *Deep Ministry in a Shallow World* (Grand Rapids: Zondervan, 2006), and also *Deep Justice* (2008). For curriculum utilizing this framework, see Kara Powell and Brad M. Griffin, *Deep Justice Journeys* (Grand Rapids: Zondervan, 2009) and Kara Powell, *Essential Leadership* (2010).

2. How Do I See Myself after Graduation?

1. Tim Clydesdale, *The First Year Out: Understanding American Teens after High School* (University of Chicago Press, 2007).

5. How Can My Struggles Help My Faith Stick?

1. Fuller Youth Institute College Transition Project, see stickyfaith.org and *Sticky Faith: Youth Worker Edition*.
2. For example, see Gay Holcomb and Arthur Nonneman, "Faithful Change: Exploring and assessing faith development in Christian liberal arts undergraduates," in Dalton et al (eds), *Assessing Character Outcomes in College* (San Francisco: Jossey-Bass, 2004, New Directions for Institutional Research No. 122, 93-103).
3. For a very helpful introduction to Psalms of lament, see Walter Brueggemann, *The Message of the Psalms: A theological commentary* (Augsburg Old Testament Studies; Minneapolis: Augsburg, 1984).

6. How Can My Friends Help My Faith Stick?

1. Fuller Youth Institute, College Transition Project, see stickyfaith.org and *Sticky Faith: Youth Worker Edition*.
2. Fuller Youth Institute, College Transition Project, see stickyfaith.org and *Sticky Faith: Youth Worker Edition*.

7. How Will I Respond to the Party Scene in College?

1. Fuller Youth Institute, College Transition Project, see stickyfaith.org and *Sticky Faith: Youth Worker Edition*.

8. How Can I Find a New Church?

1. See the Introduction for more detail. This estimate has been extrapolated from several sources: Barna Update, "Most Twentysomethings Put Christianity on the Shelf Following Spiritually Active Teen Years." *The Barna Group*, 2006, September 16, 2006; George H. Gallup, Jr., *The Gallup Poll*, 2006; and Christian Smith with Patricial Snell, *Souls in Transition* (New York: Oxford University Press, 2009), 105, 108, 109, and 116.
2. Fuller Youth Institute College Transition Project, see stickyfaith.org and *Sticky Faith: Youth Worker Edition*.
3. Fuller Youth Institute College Transition Project, see stickyfaith.org and *Sticky Faith: Youth Worker Edition*.
4. Fuller Youth Institute College Transition Project, see stickyfaith.org and *Sticky Faith: Youth Worker Edition*.

9. How Can I Manage My Life after High School?

1. Fuller Youth Institute, College Transition Project, see stickyfaith.org and *Sticky Faith: Youth Worker Edition*.
2. Public Agenda, "With Their Whole Lives Ahead of Them," December 2009 report. http://www.publicagenda.org/files/pdf/theirwholelivesaheadofthem.pdf
3. Fuller Youth Institute, College Transition Project, see stickyfaith.org and *Sticky Faith: Youth Worker Edition*.
4. Adapted from Stephen R. Covey, A. Roger Merrill and Rebecca Merrill, *First Things First: Coping with the ever-increasing demands of the workplace* (London: Simon & Schuster, 1994).

10. How Can I Experience God on a Regular Basis?

1. Fuller Youth Institute College Transition Project, see stickyfaith.org and *Sticky Faith: Youth Worker Edition*.

2. This description of *holy leisure* is from Mark Yaconelli, *Downtime: Helping Teenagers Pray* (Grand Rapids: Youth Specialties/Zondervan, 2008), 23.
3. Mother Teresa, quoted in Malcolm Muggeridge, *Something Beautiful for God* (Ballantine Books, 1979), 48.

Sticky Faith Parent Curriculum DVD

Everyday Ideas to Build Lasting Faith in Your Kids

Author: Kara E. Powell

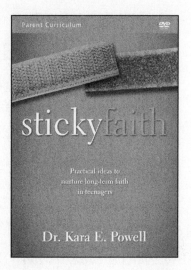

Most parents would give anything to anchor their children with a vibrant faith that "sticks" and continues to mature into adulthood. Yet, despite this deep desire, research indicates that approximately 40-50 percent of high school seniors drift from their faith after graduation.

The *Sticky Faith Parent Curriculum* is a video-based study that came from Kara Powell's desire to see her own kids emerge from adolescence with their faith intact. Through personal, real-world experiences of research and sharing, the *Sticky Faith Parent Curriculum* enables parents to instill a deep and lasting faith in their adolescents.

This video curriculum presents powerful strategies and practical ideas to help parents encourage their children's spiritual growth, enabling them to develop a faith that sticks.

Sticky Faith:
Youth Worker Edition

Practical Ideas to Nurture Long-Term Faith in Teenagers

Kara E. Powell, Brad M. Griffin and Cheryl A. Crawford

Many of the statistics you read about teenagers and faith can be alarming. Recent studies show that 40-50 percent of kids who are connected to a youth group throughout their senior year will fail to stick with their faith in college. As youth workers are pouring their time and energy into the students in their ministries, they are often left wondering if they've done enough to equip their students to carry their faith into adulthood.

Fuller Youth Institute has done extensive research in the area of youth ministry and teenage development. In *Sticky Faith: Youth Worker Edition*, the team at FYI presents youth workers with both a theological/philosophical framework and practical programming ideas that develop long-term faith in teenagers. Each chapter presents a summary of FYI's quantitative and qualitative research, along with the implications of this research, including program ideas suggested and tested by youth ministries nationwide.

This resource will give youth pastors what they need to help foster a faith that sticks with all the teenagers in their group long after they've left the youth room.

Deep Justice in a Broken World

Helping Your Kids Serve Others and Right the Wrongs around Them

Chap Clark and Kara E. Powell from the Center for Youth and Family Ministry

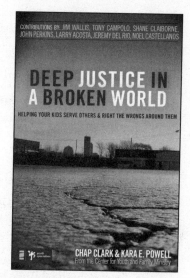

It doesn't take a long list of statistics to convince you that our world is broken. Mission trips, service projects, and supporting children through relief organizations are just a few of the ways that many youth workers engage their students in serving the least, the last, and the lost. As good and helpful as these things may be on the surface, that's where they remain—at the surface. The problems run far deeper than an occasional paint job or fundraising project can solve. But it's not hopeless. Deep social justice is possible in your youth ministry.

Following their bestselling book, *Deep Ministry in a Shallow World*, Kara Powell and Chap Clark provide you with research and insights that will help your ministry get to the next level. Their practical Kingdom of God theology will help you go beyond simply trying to motivate your students to serve those in need, and invite your students (and maybe even your leaders) to wrestle with why those people are in need in the first place. You'll hear from well-known social justice leaders and youth workers who are making a difference in urban, suburban, and small town settings including Jim Wallis, Tony Campolo, John Perkins, Shane Claiborne, and more.

In addition to expanding your personal justice commitments, *Deep Justice in a Broken World* will help you reflect with your own leadership team, and will provide you with online resources to take you even deeper into the journey.

So go ahead, dig deeper into what it means to heal the broken world in which we live. Take your ministry deeper into social justice.

Available in stores and online!

ZONDERVAN®
.com

Share Your Thoughts

With the Author: Your comments will be forwarded to
the author when you send them to *zauthor@zondervan.com*.

With Zondervan: Submit your review of this book
by writing to *zreview@zondervan.com*.

Free Online Resources at
www.zondervan.com

Zondervan AuthorTracker: Be notified whenever your favorite
authors publish new books, go on tour, or post an update
about what's happening in their lives at www.zondervan.com/
authortracker.

Daily Bible Verses and Devotions: Enrich your life with daily
Bible verses or devotions that help you start every morning
focused on God. Visit www.zondervan.com/newsletters.

Free Email Publications: Sign up for newsletters on Christian
living, academic resources, church ministry, fiction, children's
resources, and more. Visit www.zondervan.com/newsletters.

Zondervan Bible Search: Find and compare Bible passages in
a variety of translations at www.zondervanbiblesearch.com.

Other Benefits: Register to receive online benefits like
coupons and special offers, or to participate in research.

ZONDERVAN.com/
AUTHORTRACKER
follow your favorite authors